THE

GUIDE TO
HEALTHY
EATING

ROZ DENNY

MARTIN BOOKS

CONTENTS

Published by Martin Books
in cooperation with British Alcan Consumer Products Ltd

Simon & Schuster International Group
Fitzwilliam House
32 Trumpington Street
Cambridge CB2 1QY

First published 1989
© Woodhead-Faulkner (Publishers) Ltd, 1989

ISBN 0 85941 572 4

INTRODUCTION

So you're a self-confessed Glutton, who enjoys eating and drinking, and you want to continue to do so for a lot longer. You like to eat lots of nice food and drink some alcohol, but you also want to fit in somewhere along the line – but not too obtrusively – the health educator's message about eating what is good for you.

Healthy eating doesn't mean meagre portions, fibre with everything and lettuce leaves and prunes at least once a day. You don't have to wave goodbye for all time to chocolate, crisps and chips. If you are not too excessive with food, you can safely ignore the pleadings of health food fanatics who tell you that in time you'll get used to their 'brown rice, chew-for-ever and swallow-when-you-like diet'. Why go through the agony when it's not necessary? There are thousands of wonderful foods, recipes and meals that, provided they are combined cleverly to produce a balanced diet, fit all the modern criteria for healthy eating – and taste great too.

So, how to get to this state of nirvana? The answer is simple – know a bit about the foods to play up, the foods to play down and take any changes slowly, so that you can stick at it.

GLUTTONS' GUIDELINES

☞ Play up high-fibre foods

☞ Play down fats

Increase your food repertoire

Fibre is important in its own right, but it's also true that many fibre-rich foods are lower in calories. And they are filling – great news for gluttons. Nearly all fruits and vegetables fall into this 'play up' category – the exceptions are avocados and olives. Eat them in moderation because they contain a high level of fat.

Other high-fibre foods are pastas, breads, pulses and rices. They are versatile, virtually fat-free, contain lots of filling starch (now a nutrition 'goodie') with practically no salt or sugar. Just don't overload them with fats and the like when you cook.

Fatty foods to play down are pretty obvious – butter, margarine, some cheeses, oils, meat fat, meat products like sausages, cream, full cream milk, biscuits, pastry, nuts and fried foods.

There is no way anyone can make decent chips without using fat, but it's amazing how little fat many recipes actually need. For instance, fry chips at a good high temperature, which cuts down on their absorption of oil, and thicken white sauces with cornflour, not butter and flour.

FATS

There are double the amount of calories in fats as there are in proteins and starches – 9 calories per gram to be precise. So it makes sense to limit the total amount of fats and foods with high percentages of fats, such as fatty red meats, poultry skin, cakes and pastries in your diet.

The COMA report recommended that no one over five years of age should eat more than 35% of their energy as fat. For women and girls over the age of five that means no more than 60–85 g of fat a day, and boys of six and over and men, 70–110 g a day. To help you work out approximately how much fat you take in, an ounce (25 g) of hard cheese has 8 g of fat, an ounce of butter or margarine 20 g and a normal portion of chips, 16 g. Fortunately, many more lower fat spreads, cheeses and other products are coming onto the market, and manufacturers are printing fat contents on the side of their packs to help us keep track.

It is also worth remembering that hard and soft margarines and oils labelled 'low in polyunsaturates' will still be as high in calories as saturated fats. If you wish to reduce calories, then use low fat-spreads – of which there is an increasing and varied range on the market now.

If there is one golden rule about healthier eating, it is to limit the amount of fats you eat and increase fibre-rich foods such as whole grains, pulses, fruit and vegetables. Do that and continue to eat normally but moderately with a good cross-section of foods, and you'll find being a healthy glutton is more than possible.

LOWER-FAT ROASTS

Brush the surface of the meat or poultry with sunflower oil, and place it in a roasting pan with about 450 ml (¾ pint) stock or water. Cover with foil and roast as usual, uncovering for the last 20 minutes to brown.

Be adventurous The best news of all is that we should *increase* the variety of our diet. There's been so much publicity recently about fats and fibre that we tend to forget we need 13 vitamins and dozens of minerals, as well as protein and enough energy from food. If you go short of any of these, you'll suffer for it, no matter how high in fibre or low in fat your food may be. No one food contains all the nutrients we need, so the wider the variety of foods we eat, the greater the chance of getting everything we need.

A CHANGE FOR THE BETTER

Slowly change your eating habits. A gentle approach is likely to bring lasting benefits.

Stage 1: Buy and eat at least one new food a week, but not a new type of biscuit, mind you! Try different fruits, vegetables, fishes, breads and pulses.

Stage 2: Work out your fat intake, approximately. Cut down on it, if necessary, and change over to polyunsaturates, where possible, without sacrificing flavour.

Concentrate on these two objectives until you can accommodate them without thinking twice. Then move on to the next three stages.

Stage 3: How is your weight? All you need is a mirror to tell you whether you need to lose weight. If you don't like what you see, reduce high-calorie foods such as fats.

Stage 4: Take it easy on alcohol. Apart from its fattening property, excess alcohol is not good for your liver, brain or sex life. Consult page 92 for a suggested weekly intake of alcohol.

Stage 5: Finally, go easy on salt (page 48) and sugar. Again, don't rush at this. Cut down gradually and the chances are you'll stick at it.

ACKNOWLEDGEMENT

Grateful thanks to consultant nutritionist Jenny Salmon, for her sensible and enthusiastic help with this book.

Roz Denny

NOTES

Ingredients are given in both metric and imperial measures. Use either set of quantities, but not a mixture of both, in any one recipe.

All spoon measurements are level:

1 tablespoon = one 15 ml spoon
1 teaspoon = one 5 ml spoon

Eggs are standard (size 3) unless otherwise stated.

The symbol denotes that the dish, although good for you, is still quite high in calories, so go easy!

GET SET

Start the day off well

We used to be encouraged to start the day 'with a good breakfast'. Those who felt unable to face food before midday must have wondered if they were only firing on half their cylinders.

Now, nutritionists are more relaxed about it. You do not *have* to eat if you function quite well without food in the morning, but it is still a good idea to have something, if only to stop you stuffing a mid-morning chocolate bar.

Also, many breakfast foods are excellent sources of dietary fibre. A good helping of a high-bran cereal can give you up to half your daily needs. Use skimmed or semi-skimmed milk and top with sliced fresh fruit for an excellent breakfast. Or try a couple of slices of wholemeal toast, lightly spread with low-fat spread and topped with some thin slices of a medium-fat cheese, like Edam, followed by fresh fruit.

Breakfast-in-a-Glass

If you can't face eating but don't mind drinking, then try the following. Put into a food processor or blender 200 ml (7 fl oz) of your favourite fruit juice, 1 egg, 1 small ripe banana, 2 tablespoons of natural yogurt, and 2 teaspoons wheatgerm. Whizz it all up until it is smooth and creamy, and serve it over crushed ice if the weather outside merits it.

Muesli

If you have always wanted to make your own muesli, then first find yourself a good health food shop because it will stock an interesting selection of grains and flakes. Also, mixing your own muesli means you can control the sugar levels and choose your own mix of fruits. I know someone who painstakingly picks out and discards every raisin from his bowl each morning. If he made his own, he could have another five minutes in bed each day!

Here is a suggestion for proportions of cereals and a list of fruits – so carry on and mix and match. Remember, muesli (even without sugar) is quite high in calories, but because it takes such a long time to chew each mouthful you do not need quite as much.

For the base:
250 g (8 oz) rolled or porridge oats
125 g (4 oz) jumbo oats
125 g (4 oz) barley flakes
125 g (4 oz) rye flakes
125 g (4 oz) hazelnuts, halved, or almond flakes, toasted lightly
50 g (2 oz) desiccated coconut, toasted lightly
50 g (2 oz) raw brown sugar (optional)
1 teaspoon mixed spice (optional)
Extras:
Add your favourite dried fruits (chopped up if necessary), such as raisins, apricots, peaches, dates, banana chips, pears and pineapple. Exact quantities depend on your own taste.

Mix all the ingredients together and store in an airtight jar. The addition of spice makes it quite unusual and is particularly delicious when hot milk is added.

You could make up double or treble quantity and store the excess in Alcan food bags, sealing with a twisted bag tag. In fact, bags of your own special mix muesli would make super personal presents, especially if you are going to stay with friends or family for a weekend.

Allow about 4–6 tablespoons of mix at a time, and eat with skimmed or semi-skimmed milk, or try it with buttermilk, or fruit juice, or even your own home-made soft yogurt. Some people like to soften muesli first in milk or juice for half an hour.

Dried Apricot Jam

This is actually a purée of dried apricots, and it can be used as a substitute for jam or marmalade at breakfast. It has the advantage of being high in fibre and there is no added sugar. The orange-flower-water is a touch exotic, but if you can find it, (in delicatessens) it is an interesting addition. The jam only keeps for a fortnight in the fridge, so if your family are slow jam-eaters, store half in the freezer in a freezerproof container covered with Bacofoil for up to 3 months.

Makes 1.5 kg (3½ lb)
500 g (1 lb) no-soak dried apricots
1.2 litres (2 pints) water
grated rind and juice of 2 oranges
1 teaspoon triple-strength orange-flower-water (optional)

1 Chop the apricots and place in a saucepan with the water, orange rind and juice.
2 Bring to the boil, cover and simmer gently for about 40 minutes until thick and pulpy. Uncover and bubble off excess liquid if the mixture is not thick enough.
3 Stir in the orange-flower-water, if used, and spoon while still hot into sterilised glass jam jars, or cool a little and store in plastic food containers.

Breakfast-in-a-glass; Muesli, with dried fruits; Dried Apricot Jam;
American Pumpkin Bran Muffins

American Pumpkin Bran Muffins

Wonderful for winter weekend brunches when pumpkins are plentiful. Freshly baked, these can be eaten without any butter or jam, although they do taste even more delicious with a *thin* spreading of each.

Makes 12

margarine, for greasing
125 g (4 oz) plain flour
125 g (4 oz) wholemeal flour
2 teaspoons baking powder
2 teaspoons mixed spice
2 tablespoons bran
50 g (2 oz) soft brown sugar
grated rind of 1 orange
50 g (2 oz) raisins or chopped walnuts
2 eggs, beaten
1 tablespoon sunflower oil
125 ml (4 fl oz) skimmed milk
175 g (6 oz) fresh or canned pumpkin purée

1 Lightly grease a 12-section muffin or deep bun tin. Preheat the oven to Gas Mark 6/200°C/400°F.

2 Sift the dry ingredients (except for the bran) into a large bowl. Tip all the bran, including any from sifting the flour, into a bowl. Mix in the sugar, orange rind, and raisins or walnuts.

3 Beat the eggs, oil, milk and pumpkin purée together. Then mix into the dry ingredients lightly and quickly without overmixing.

4 Spoon into the bun tins and bake for about 25 minutes until risen and firm.

5 Cool a little in the tins. Then turn out and serve while still warm.

Note: These can be cooled and frozen in freezer bags for up to 1 month. Reheat in a warm oven before serving.

Paw Paw Salad with Honey Yogurt

An exotic, but simple to prepare, special breakfast salad. Make sure the paw paw (papaya) is quite ripe. Ideally, use Greek yogurt, or fromage frais.

Serves 2

1 large ripe paw paw, halved, peeled and de-seeded
2 kiwifruits, peeled and halved
4 tablespoons yogurt, preferably Greek
1–3 teaspoons clear honey
a pinch of ground cinnamon
a few flaked almonds, toasted

1 Cut the fruits into elegant slices and arrange on two small plates.
2 Mix the yogurt with honey, to taste, and the cinnamon.
3 Spoon into the middle of the fruits and sprinkle with some almonds, to garnish.

Low-sugar Peach Jam

Low-sugar jams need to be made with pulpy fruits if they are not to be too runny. You also need the commercial setting agent, Certo, to give the jam some body. This jam can also be made with nectarines.

Makes 1.1 kg (2½ lb)

1 kg (2 lb) peaches or nectarines, halved, stoned and chopped
juice of ½ lemon
250 g (8 oz) granulated sugar
125 ml (4 fl oz) Certo

1 Gently simmer the fruit with the lemon juice in a large thick-based saucepan, for 15–20 minutes, until softened and the juice runs.
2 Add the sugar and stir until it is dissolved. Then bring to a full rolling boil. Boil rapidly for 7 minutes, timing from when the mixture starts to boil well.
3 Remove from the heat and stir in the Certo. Put in clean, sterilised glass jars and cover either with jam pot covers or vacuum-seal twist jar tops. Cool and store in the fridge, and use within 3 weeks.

Grill-up

When you have the time and are inclined to decadence, a traditional cooked breakfast is hard to resist. However, there is no need to bring out the frying pan; if you grill them, you can serve almost the same foods as in a fry-up, saying 'No' only to fried bread and black pudding. Here is a lower-fat version of Britain's favourite breakfast.

Serves 2

2 lamb's kidneys, skinned, halved and cored, or 2 thin slices lamb's liver
a little olive oil
3 chipolata sausages, halved
2 large tomatoes, halved
a good pinch of dried mixed herbs or thyme
2 lean rashers back bacon, fat removed
4 slices french bread, preferably wholemeal
1 garlic clove, halved
2 open-cup mushrooms
1 teaspoon coarse-grain mustard
2 eggs (optional)
salt and ground black pepper

1 Lay the kidneys or liver on the grill pan and brush very lightly with some of the olive oil. Add the sausages and tomatoes, season lightly and sprinkle with a little of the herbs. Grill for about 5 minutes, turning the kidneys or liver and sausages (liver may not need as long). Remove and keep warm.
2 Grill the bacon for 3 minutes. The bacon should not need turning unless it is quite thick. Remove and keep warm.
3 Toast the bread lightly on both sides. Then rub one side with the cut clove of garlic and brush with a very light film of olive oil. Keep warm too.
4 The mushrooms should be poached in a little water in a small covered saucepan, with the herbs and coarse-grain mustard, for about 3 minutes.
5 If using eggs, poach these in water that is just simmering and drain well on kitchen towel.
6 Now serve the whole lot together on two plates.

Veggie Kedgie

The Indian dish on which our classic breakfast haddock and rice kedgeree is based was called 'kitchiri' – made of rice, lentils and spices. Lentils, as we know, are bouncing with protein and fibre and are therefore a good option for vegetarians, who have a limited choice of cooked breakfasts. This dish can be made in advance; then just reheat and add the eggs when you tumble out of bed in the morning.

GET SET

Serves 4

125 g (4 oz) lentils, brown, green or red
2 bay leaves
1 vegetable stock cube, dissolved (optional)
1 onion, chopped
1 garlic clove, crushed
2 tablespoons sunflower oil
1 teaspoon mild curry powder
125 g (4 oz) button mushrooms, sliced
175 g (6 oz) brown rice
1 egg
salt and ground black pepper
2 hard-boiled eggs and 1 tablespoon chopped fresh parsley, to garnish

1 If using brown or green lentils, cover and soak overnight in cold water. Red lentils need no soaking. Drain, cover in water in a saucepan, add the bay leaves and bring to the boil.
2 Simmer with the lid on for 30 minutes for brown and green lentils, or 20 minutes for red. Drain, reserve the water, stir in the stock cube, and make it up to 600 ml (1 pint) with more water.
3 Fry the onion and garlic in the oil for about 5 minutes, until softened. Add the curry powder and mushrooms and cook for 2 minutes.
4 Fry the rice in the pan for a minute or two before pouring in the stock, if using. Season lightly, bring to the boil and turn down to a gentle simmer.
5 Cook for about 45 minutes (easy-cook rice will only need about 30 minutes).
6 The liquid should all have been absorbed. If not, cook uncovered for a few minutes until it has been.
7 Stir in the beaten egg – this makes it creamy and it cooks lightly in the heat. Then serve straightaway, garnished with the hard-boiled eggs, sliced or chopped, and the parsley.

A Dish of Mustardy Kidneys

Reminiscent of old country-house cooking, where no breakfast was complete without a dish of kidneys, this recipe is perfect for today's weekend brunches; particularly as kidneys are an excellent source of iron. If you can find them, use veal kidneys, which are tender and sweet. Otherwise, lamb's kidneys are almost as good.

Serves 2

250 g (8 oz) veal or lamb's kidneys
15 g (½ oz) butter
1 tablespoon sunflower oil
juice and 1 teaspoon grated rind of 1 small orange
1–2 teaspoons coarse-grain mustard
2 tablespoons dry sherry or water
2 tablespoons fromage frais
1 tablespoon chopped fresh parsley
salt and ground black pepper
toast and tomato quarters, to serve

1 Peel the membranes from the kidneys, and use kitchen scissors to cut out the core. Cut into 1 cm (½-inch) slices.

2 In a heavy-based frying pan, heat the butter and oil until the foaming ceases. Then fry the kidney slices for 2–3 minutes until just done, turning once. Take care not to overcook or they will be tough.

3 Add the orange juice and rind, mustard and sherry or water, and stir to blend. Simmer for a minute or two until reduced by a half, then stir in the fromage frais, seasoning and parsley. Serve hot with triangles of toast and some tomato quarters.

COOKING VEGETABLES

Cook, when necessary, as quickly and lightly as possible, and always in the minimum amount of water. Two of the main vegetable vitamins, B and C, are water-soluble, that is, they leak out into the cooking water, so use the cooking liquor in gravy, sauces, casseroles, and so on, instead of throwing it down the sink. Microwave and oven|cooking are excellent ways of retaining the nutrients.

Green vegetables and those best served crisp, such as cauliflower, sweetcorn and courgettes, can be cooked in foil parcels; cut into even-sized pieces, add a tablespoon or two of water and a knob of butter or low-fat spread, then wrap tightly and cook on a baking sheet at about Gas Mark 5/190°C/375°F for 20–25 minutes, until just tender.

GET SET

ON THE GO

Light meals in moments

The traditional three-meals-a-day eating pattern is supposed to be declining – we are all far too busy rushing around to sit down and eat together. Instead, we can have up to six eating 'occasions' a day, ranging from little nibbles to perhaps one main meal. It is all too tempting to stuff a doughnut or rush to the nearest take-away for a burger. So, here are some ideas for simple, tasty, in-between fillers that can also provide you with a lot of good nutrition.

Let us start with some trusted favourites. Bread is an excellent food, especially if it is wholemeal, which is good news for sandwich and toast fanatics (page 43). Try avoiding butter or hard margarine and change to one of the new low-fat spreads. Then spread or top your bread with foods high in protein, fibre, vitamins and minerals. Such a snack can be almost as good for you as a full-blown meal. Baked beans on toast, for instance, is an excellent protein- and fibre-packed meal for those 'on the go'.

Other simple quick snack foods ideal for healthy gluttons include:

☛ **Microwave baked potatoes** take 5–7 minutes to cook, on average. Avoid butter and try filling with these alternatives: some low-fat cheese; a flavoured cottage cheese; baked beans; a little diced corned beef; flaked smoked mackerel; cooked haddock; or some low-fat liver pâté.

☛ **Pizza-style muffins** split and lightly toasted. Top with sliced tomato, thinly sliced onion rings, some grated Edam or mozzarella cheese, sliced black olives, a couple of thin slices of salami (chopped up) and a sprinkle of dried marjoram or oregano. Pop back under the grill to reheat and melt the cheese.

☛ **Corny chicken toasts** made by mixing diced, cold, leftover chicken with some sweetcorn (or leftover peas) and a small dollop of reduced-calorie mayonnaise. Reheat under the grill.

☛ **Mushrooms and green garlic cream** using sliced button mushrooms. Poach the mushrooms in a little stock. Then stir in a little low-fat soft cheese or semi-skimmed soft cheese (quark), a squirt of garlic purée or a clove of crushed garlic and some chopped fresh parsley. Spoon into a small bowl and eat with fingers of toast.

☛ **Recycled salads** are easily put together from whatever cold vegetables, pasta or rice are in the fridge. Try mixing with a little vinaigrette and either diced, cold roast meat, or ham, or a small can of tuna, sardines or pilchards. Serve attractively on a lettuce leaf with maybe a few slices of cucumber and tomato; enjoy it with a crunchy crispbread as well.

Egg and Bacon Pasta

I like to experiment with some popular recipes until I find a version that suits us well. This is a favourite variation of spaghetti carbonara which I used to introduce my children to wholemeal pasta. The creamy egg gets caught up in the shells and the bacon stays crisp and well distributed. I think that fresh parmesan is best for this or, if you can get it, the ewe's milk cheese, pecorino. They are both quite strong, so a little goes a long way.

Serves 3–4
175 g (6 oz) wholemeal pasta shells
4–6 rashers lean bacon, de-rinded
1 tablespoon olive oil, preferably extra-virgin
1 garlic clove, crushed (optional)
2 eggs, beaten
25 g (1 oz) fresh mature parmesan or pecorino cheese, grated
ground black pepper and freshly ground nutmeg

1 Cook the pasta in plenty of boiling water until just cooked, but still with some texture. Times vary according to brands, so check the pack for instructions. Drain and rinse in hot water.
2 Meanwhile, fry the bacon in the oil with the garlic (if using) until crisp. Then remove with a slotted spoon and drain on kitchen paper.
3 Toss the pasta into the pan with the bacon oil and stir until well coated. Season with pepper and nutmeg and reheat.
4 Beat the eggs again with the seasoning and stir into the pasta when off the heat. The mixture should go creamy as the heat of the pasta will be sufficient to cook it lightly.
5 Serve immediately on heated plates, sprinkled with cheese and bacon.

ON THE GO

Chilli Liver on Rye

A quick sauté of sliced lamb's liver served on rye bread toast is an excellent power-packed snack lunch.

Serves 2

125 g (4 oz) lamb's liver, sliced thinly
1 tablespoon wholemeal flour
a good pinch of chilli powder and ground cumin
a good pinch of oregano (optional)
1 tablespoon sunflower oil
3 spring onions, sliced
2 teaspoons tomato chilli relish
juice of ½ lemon
2 slices rye bread
salt and ground black pepper
a little chopped fresh parsley, to garnish

1 Put the liver, flour, spices, oregano (if used) and a little seasoning into a food bag and shake well. Remove and shake off any excess flour.
2 Heat the oil in a small saucepan and stir-fry the liver with the spring onions for about 3 minutes until just cooked. Stir in the relish and sprinkle in the lemon juice.
3 Meanwhile, toast the bread and serve the liver straightaway on both slices, garnished with some parsley.

Roz's Ratatouille

Being a natural peasant at heart, I am a great one for stew things in pots. Ratatouille is one of those pot meals that can be made in bulk and stored in the fridge for a few days. It becomes a great base for many types of meals, being sufficiently adaptable to be added to as you use it up. It is also an excellent healthy base for single people who want to eat well without having to live on snacks.

Here are just some of the ways in which I have used it (hot and cold), ranging from the days when I lived in a bedsit on my own through to family meals:

- ☛ sprinkled lightly with grated cheese
- ☛ served with either poached eggs or hard-boiled eggs
- ☛ with added cooked, dried beans, such as red kidney beans
- ☛ with chopped, cold leftover meat and poultry
- ☛ with cooked white fish

- with brown rice and nuts
- with wholemeal pasta shapes
- with a lovely warm crusty wholemeal roll in front of the television!

The secret, I find, is to make it the day before I intend to start eating a batch and to let the flavours mature. I only cook the vegetables lightly since they soften more while cooling, yet still retain an interesting texture. Also, I avoid sticking rigidly to this one recipe – it varies according to what I find lurking in the fridge salad drawer – mushrooms, leeks, peas and even diced swede and parsnips have found their way into the ratatouille pot over the years. And nowadays, I do allow myself the luxury of using the best quality extra-virgin olive oil I can find – it does help the flavour.

Makes enough for 8 pot-meals

1 large aubergine, cut into chunks
1 large onion, sliced
2 garlic cloves, crushed
3 tablespoons olive oil, preferably extra-virgin
1 large red or green pepper, cored and sliced
750 g (1½ lb) courgettes, sliced thickly
150 ml (¼ pint) dry white wine, for special occasions (optional)
2 × 400 g (14 oz) can of chopped tomatoes
2 tablespoons chopped fresh oregano or marjoram or 1 teaspoon dried oregano or marjoram
1 large sprig of fresh thyme or small one of fresh rosemary (optional)
3 tablespoons chopped fresh parsley
salt and ground black pepper

1 Sprinkle the aubergine chunks lightly with salt in a colander. Then leave to drain in the sink for about 20 minutes. Rinse the chunks and pat them dry with a kitchen towel.
2 Gently fry the onion, garlic and aubergine in the oil in a large pan for about 10 minutes. It helps to cover them with a lid since this stops the steam from drying out and prevents the oil from being absorbed too much by the aubergines.
3 Add the pepper and courgettes and cook for another 5 minutes. If using wine, then cook this at the same time to allow it to reduce.
4 Add the rest of the ingredients, season lightly, cover, and cook for a further 5 minutes. Cool and leave at least overnight.

Cheesy Two-bean Toasts

A popular Stateside version of beans on toast.

Serves 2–4
1 small onion, sliced
1 garlic clove, crushed
1 small green pepper, de-seeded and sliced thinly
1 tablespoon sunflower oil
200 g (7 oz) can of baked beans
200 g (7 oz) can of red kidney or butter beans
1 tablespoon tomato ketchup
1 teaspoon Worcestershire sauce
4 slices wholemeal bread, or 2 muffins, split
50 g (2 oz) mature cheese, grated finely
ground black pepper

1 Fry the onion, garlic and pepper in the oil for about 3 minutes, until softened.
2 Add the beans, ketchup, sauce and pepper. Heat until just bubbling.
3 Meanwhile, toast the bread or muffins on both sides. Spoon over the beans.
4 Sprinkle the cheese over the beans and return to the grill until the cheese is bubbling and golden.

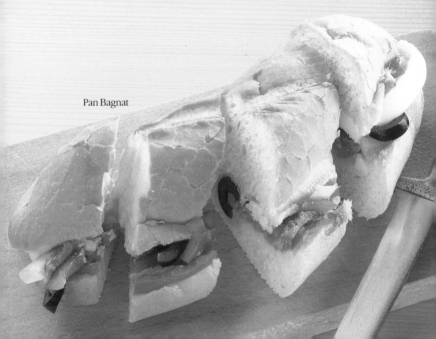

Pan Bagnat

a-style Muffins (page 16)

Cheesy Two-bean Toasts

Pan Bagnat

This is a Mediterranean speciality originating from Nice, a sort of *Salade Niçoise* in a bun. Ideal for a light meal on a hot summer's day – when we get one.

Serves 4

4 crusty baps or long rolls
1 garlic clove, halved
4 tablespoons extra-virgin olive oil
2 tablespoons red wine vinegar
2 ripe tomatoes, sliced thinly
2 hard-boiled eggs, sliced thinly
¼ small green pepper, sliced thinly
a few thinly sliced onion rings or 2 spring onions, chopped
50 g (2 oz) can of anchovy fillets, drained and chopped
1 tablespoon chopped fresh parsley or basil
about 8 black olives, stoned and sliced
salt and ground black pepper

1 Slice the baps or rolls in half, and rub them with the garlic clove.
2 Make a simple dressing with the oil, vinegar and some seasoning and dribble this on the cut sides of the rolls.
3 Lay all the ingredients inside the rolls. Close the rolls tightly and wrap each well and tightly in Bacofoil, the idea being that the dressing and ingredients fuse together. Pack them closely together in a box.
4 Chill for about 3 hours in the fridge. Then unwrap and serve each roll sliced in four.

Your Own Freezer Fishcakes

This is about the only recipe I still use deep-frying for, because you do need to get a good seal on the coating. However, the fishcakes are only immersed briefly in the oil; the actual cooking is done under the grill or in the oven.

Makes 18

500 g (1 lb) filleted and skinned white fish, e.g. cod, haddock, coley, etc.
250 g (8 oz) filleted and skinned smoked haddock or cod
1 kg (2 lb) floury potatoes, e.g. Edwards, Maris Piper, reds
3 spring onions, chopped finely
1 teacup of fresh chopped parsley or 1½ teaspoons mixed dried herbs

1 teaspoon ground mace
2 tablespoons capers, chopped (optional)
a little milk, if necessary
salt and ground black pepper
For the coating:
some wholemeal flour
2 eggs (size 1 or 2), beaten
150 g (5 oz) dried breadcrumbs, preferably your own home-made
sunflower oil, for deep-frying

1 Poach the two types of fish in a little water until just firm or about 10 minutes. Remove the fish and check for any stray bones before flaking.

2 Boil the potatoes until soft but not mushy. Drain them and mash well.

3 Mix the fish with the potatoes, spring onions, parsley or herbs, mace, capers (if used) and seasoning. The mixture should be soft but firm. If it seems a bit dry add a little milk.

4 Divide the mixture and shape it into 18 fairly thin patties. Cover them with cling film and chill.

5 Toss each patty in flour. Then coat each in beaten egg and finally in breadcrumbs. This is messy – it is best to do each stage for all the fishcakes at one go; that way the breadcrumbs do not all stick together.

6 Pour enough oil into a deep-fat-frying pan to come a third of the way up (this will be at least a litre (1¾ pints). Heat the oil to a temperature of 185°C/370°F, or until a piece of white bread browns in under a minute.

7 Fry the cakes (about 3 at a time) until they are just golden brown and sealed – for about a minute. Remove them and drain well. Seal the other cakes, reheating the oil in between batches.

8 Cool the cakes and then open-freeze on a wire tray. Wrap each cake individually in cling film or Bacofoil and keep them all together in a food bag.

9 To cook from frozen, unwrap the cakes when you are ready for a quick meal. If you only want one or two cakes, then grill under a medium heat for about 3 to 4 minutes each side. Batches of cakes can be cooked on a baking sheet in the oven at Gas Mark 5/190°C/375°F for about 20 minutes.

FISH

It is high in first class protein, and white fish is also very low in fat. Oily fish (such as herrings, mackerel and salmon) contain certain unsaturated fats, and there is evidence that the oil in fish can help prevent heart disease.

Microwaving fish is an excellent way of cooking it: simply place in a shallow, non-metallic ovenproof dish, season lightly, dress with some fresh lemon juice, a pinch of herbs and a little oil, if liked, then cover with microwave cooking film, pierced a few times. Cook according to your oven's instruction manual.

Chinese Vegetable Omelette

Eggs and tasty vegetables are classic Chinese cuisine; they are also very quick.

ON THE GO

Serves 2

3 eggs, beaten
2 tablespoons water
2 tablespoons sunflower oil
2 spring onions, chopped
1 garlic clove, crushed
1 small knob of fresh root ginger, peeled and chopped
1 carrot, grated
125 g (4 oz) button mushrooms, sliced
50 g (2 oz) fresh beanshoots
1 tablespoon dry sherry (optional)
1 tablespoon light soy sauce
salt and ground black pepper

1 Beat the eggs and water with some seasoning. Set aside.

2 Heat half the oil in a medium-size frying pan and stir-fry the onions, garlic, ginger and carrot for 2 minutes. ·

3 Add the mushrooms and beanshoots, stir-frying for a further minute. Pour over the sherry, if used, and the soy sauce. Season with some pepper only. Remove with a slotted spoon.

4 Heat the remaining oil until it is quite hot and pour in the beaten egg. Make an omelette and, when nearly set, return the vegetables. Flip over one side and cut in two. Serve on warm plates, immediately. This is good with some leftover rice.

Eggs Lucullus

Serves 4

1 tablespoon olive or sunflower oil
125 g (4 oz) button mushrooms, sliced
1 small Cos or round lettuce, shredded
1 garlic clove, crushed
1 tablespoon chopped fresh parsley
4 eggs
25 g (1 oz) mature Cheddar cheese, grated finely
salt, ground black pepper and ground nutmeg

1 In a shallow flameproof pan, e.g. a French cast-iron gratin dish, heat the oil and gently fry the mushrooms, lettuce and garlic until just cooked. This should take about 3 minutes.

2 Season with salt, pepper and nutmeg. Then stir in the parsley.

3 Make four wells in the mixture and break an egg into each. Cover the top with a pan lid or sheet of foil and cook gently for about 3–5 minutes until the eggs are just set.

4 Sprinkle with the cheese, which should start to melt, and serve immediately.

Sprouting Beanshoots

Once you've got into the habit of sprouting your own beans and seeds they can turn quick snacks into more substantial, flavoursome and nutritious meals. They can be used:

- over scrambled eggs
- in soups (home-made and bought)
- in sandwiches and rolls
- over vegetable dishes
- on simply dressed pasta or rice
- in salads
- in stir-frys (of course!)
- sprinkled on dishes like spaghetti instead of cheese
- in stuffings
- in risottos and pilafs

Most beans and peas are suitable for sprouting and will do so readily as long as they are not too old. Germination takes 2–5 days, depending on type and the weather.

Which beans? The nicest to start with are chick-peas, green lentils (split red lentils will not sprout), mung beans and aduki beans.

The equipment is simple You will need large tall glass jars, e.g. coffee jars without their lids, cling film and elastic bands.

The method is easy Use 2–3 tablespoons of dried beans or peas at a time. Soak overnight in water, then rinse and put into a jar. Cover the top with a double sheet of cling film, stretched tight, and secure round the top with a band. Puncture a number of holes in the film with a skewer.

Lay the jar on its side and store in warm daylight but out of direct sunlight. Rinse with fresh tepid water and drain night and morning through the film top, shaking the beans gently to release any stale water. Replace the jar on its side.

The sprouts are ready when they are at least 3 times the length of the original seed. Fresh sprouts are very nutritious, being a good source of vitamin C, easy to digest, and high in fibre. So, get sprouting. Once you master the knack, you will find it easy to get into the habit, and will always have a good supply ready for instant use.

Once grown, put in a food bag and store in the fridge. Use each batch within 3 days.

Special Sardines on Toast

Spend a few more minutes jazzing up this old family favourite – it will certainly make it more substantial.

Serves 4
120 g (4 oz) can of sardines, drained
juice of ½ lemon
1 spring onion, chopped
1 tomato, chopped
4 slices granary-type or multi-grain bread
75 g (3 oz) Edam cheese, grated
ground black pepper

1 Mash the sardines with the lemon juice and black pepper. Mix with the onion and tomato.
2 Toast one side of the bread. Then spread the sardine mixture on top of the other side.
3 Sprinkle the mixture with cheese and return to the grill, cooking until the cheese is bubbling and golden. Cut each slice in half and serve immediately with some salad.

PICKERS' PARADISE

Healthy between-meal snacks

Or 'confessions of a picker' – this section is written from the heart! Pickers of the world are united in their feeding pattern – that of little and often. And nutritionists tell us that it's not at all bad as long as we pick at the right things and not too much at one time. After all, it's not so much when we eat, but what and how much, that matters most.

Things to spread or scoop up are ideal pickers' fodder – pâtés, dips, plus little bits to pop into the mouth without much effort or having to get out a spoon or fork. Half the fun of picking is opening the fridge or cupboard door and having a good sniff around. To pick healthily, simply replace foods not too good for you with foods not too bad – in moderation of course.

So keep your biscuit tin, sweetie pot, and fridge containers. They can still be filled with something crunchy and something sweet, or something creamy and good to eat.

Part of the art of picking is not necessarily making a special pickers' dish. It is just having tasty things around that need tidying up or levelling out. Here is a list of suggested useful picky bits to have on hand:

☛ **Fruit**, particularly 'pop in the mouth' fruit like grapes, cherries, apricots, little apples, and kumquats, if you enjoy the sharp flavour. Oranges are not really conducive to picking – they need too much thought and effort. Bananas are fine, but they do need to be eaten all at once, so choose small ones, as bananas are a bit higher than most fruit in calories.

☛ **Dried fruits**, like apricots, figs, no-soak prunes, plump raisins, currants, dried banana chips and the like. These are good substitutes for sweets, with useful things like minerals and fibre in them; they are still quite high in the old calories, however, so go easy – just a small fistful at a time.

☛ **Crunchy bits** such as cereals, particularly mini shredded wheats, shreddies and branflakes – but not sugar-coated cereals. Pop them into little storage jars. Also nice is crunchy oat cereal with those bits of chopped dried apple and dried fruit. Go easy on it because it does contain sugar.

☛ **Nuts and seeds** are high in calories but are also good sources of protein. Choose unsalted nuts like peanut kernels or hazelnuts and almonds. They taste even better lightly roasted before they are stored in a jar. Sunflower seeds are a great addition to the pickers' range – again roast them for an even better flavour. Because such titbits are very moreish, I find it a useful discipline to shake out a (smallish) measured amount into a ramekin dish and ration my indulgence.

☞ **Biscuits** are best for you when plain or semi-sweet, especially those high in fibre made with wholemeal flour, and preferably small in size. Digestives may be high in fibre but they are also quite high in calories so avoid them if you are slimming. Also, try and resist chocolate-coated or cream-filled biscuits, or restrict them to an occasional heavenly treat. Most semi-sweet biscuits are around 50 calories, while a chocolate-coated one is 100 calories.

☞ **Sweets** which take time to eat, like hard fruit gums, simple boiled sweets and dolly mixtures, are better for you than other kinds, although they are still quite high in calories, e.g. a boiled sweet contains 25 calories.

Tapenade

A French black olive and anchovy dip or spread that is quite highly flavoured, so a little goes a long way.

250 g (8 oz) black olives, drained if necessary
1 garlic clove, crushed
50 g (2 oz) can of anchovies, drained, rinsed and dried
2 tablespoons capers
2 tablespoons olive oil, preferably extra-virgin, plus extra for storing
ground black pepper
vegetable sticks, toast or biscuits, for serving

1 Stone the olives with a cherry stoner or cut the flesh off with a small sharp knife.
2 Put all the ingredients into a food processor or liquidiser and blend until smooth. Alternatively, for a chunkier tapenade, they can be finely chopped together or crushed using a pestle and mortar.
3 Spoon into a small bowl and keep covered with Bacofoil or cling film, resealing well each time you take some out. Eat with vegetable sticks, or spread on toast or biscuits. For storing longer than a week, cover with a thin layer of olive oil.

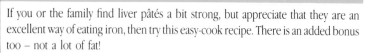

Light Lean Chicken and Liver Pâté

If you or the family find liver pâtés a bit strong, but appreciate that they are an excellent way of eating iron, then try this easy-cook recipe. There is an added bonus too – not a lot of fat!

1 onion, chopped
2 garlic cloves, crushed
4 tablespoons low-fat spread
250 g (8 oz) boned and skinned chicken breasts, diced
250 g (8 oz) chicken livers, thawed if frozen, chopped
2 tablespoons brandy or dry sherry
150 ml (¼ pint) stock
3–5 fresh sage leaves or ½ teaspoon dried sage
2 tablespoons chopped fresh marjoram or 1 teaspoon dried marjoram
salt and ground black pepper

1 Lightly sauté the onion and garlic in the low-fat spread in a frying pan for about 5 minutes.

2 Add the chicken breasts and stir-fry for 2 minutes until browned. Then add the livers and continue cooking, still stirring, for another 3 minutes.

3 Add the brandy or sherry and allow to bubble for a minute or so (this boils off the alcohol but leaves you with the flavour). Then add the stock, herbs (reserving 2 fresh sage leaves for garnishing, if you want), and seasoning.

4 Simmer for about 5 more minutes, when the meat should be just cooked but not tough.

5 Tip it all into a food processor or blender and whizz until smooth. Spoon into a bowl or 500 g (1 lb) foil dish and chill until set, garnishing with those reserved sage leaves if you feel like it. When firm, cover with Bacofoil or cling film and eat within 5 days.

Note: This can be frozen for up to a month, if wrapped in Bacofoil or cling film, but some liquid will seep out on thawing. This is harmless and the pâté just needs to be mixed together again.

Cocoa Cut 'n' bake Biscuits

These may look deathly fattening, but the idea is that you can cut the chilled dough quite thin for the best of both worlds – a good chocolate biscuit for a moderate amount of calories. Not to mention the bit of iron in the cocoa powder. They soften quite quickly once baked, but let that not be an excuse for tidying them up all at once.

The dough keeps for a while in the fridge – up to 2 weeks – so you can cut and bake in batches. Or, if you are really disciplined, freeze half for later. Incidentally, the fat needs to be of the hard type, so that the dough cuts thinly.

Makes about 48–55

100 g (4 oz) butter or hard margarine, softened
50 g (2 oz) dark brown soft sugar or molasses
75 g (3 oz) caster sugar
1 egg, beaten
1 teaspoon vanilla essence
250 g (8 oz) plain flour, plus extra for rolling
a good pinch of cream of tartar
2 tablespoons cocoa powder

1 Cream the butter or margarine together with the sugars until light and fluffy.
2 Beat in the egg and essence.
3 Sift the flour, cream of tartar and cocoa powder together and stir into the mixture until you form a firm dough.
4 On a lightly floured board, roll to a long 'sausage' about 4 cm (1½ inches) in diameter. You may find this easier to do in foil. Certainly it helps to get a nice smooth shape.
5 Cut in half if too long for your fridge shelf – half could be frozen for later. Wrap well in Bacofoil and chill until quite solid.
6 When you want to cook them, preheat the oven to Gas Mark 6/200°C/400°F. Cut wafer-thin slices of dough with a sharp knife. Rewrap the remaining dough and put it back into the fridge. It should keep for up to a fortnight, if you can make it last for that long.
7 Lay the slices on a non-stick or well-seasoned baking sheet and make a pattern on them with a fork. Then bake for about 7 minutes until just firm. Remove to a wire tray to crispen up.

PICKERS' PARADISE

The Sweetie Pot

Mid-evening is the worst time for pickers. You have had a good meal and are not really hungry, but you feel like a little something and turn to the sweet or cookie jar. *Don't!* Here is a suggested mix of sweet dried fruits and nuts that you could sit with on your lap instead. But take care not to get too carried away – they are almost as high in calories as sweets but, of course, better for you.

50 g (2 oz) unsalted peanut kernels
50 g (2 oz) dried banana chips
100 g (3½ oz) dried apricots, halved
100 g (3½ oz) dried figs, stalks snipped out and halved
100 g (3½ oz) no-soak prunes or large plump raisins

Mix everything together in a bowl. Then spoon into a large glass jar and store.

The Sweetie Pot

American Cut-'n'-come-again Carrot Cake

Cocoa Cut'n'Bake Biscuits

American Cut-'n'-come-again Carrot Cake

This cake keeps moist because of the grated carrot and apple, which means you can halve the usual amount of fat.

Makes 12–16 slices
125 g (4 oz) self-raising flour
125 g (4 oz) wholemeal flour
1½ teaspoons baking powder
1 teaspoon cinnamon
125 g (4 oz) dark soft brown sugar or molasses
175 g (6 oz) carrot, grated
1 large apple, cored and grated
50 g (2 oz) chopped walnuts
50 g (2 oz) raisins or sultanas
2 eggs, beaten
2 tablespoons sunflower oil, plus extra for greasing
grated rind and juice of 1 large orange

1 Line the base of a 1 kg (2 lb) loaf tin with Bacofoil and grease lightly. Preheat the oven to Gas Mark 3/160°C/325°F.
2 Sift the flours with the baking powder and cinnamon into a large bowl and tip in any bran left over in the sieve.
3 Mix in the sugar, carrot, apple, nuts and dried fruit. Make a well in the centre.
4 Beat the eggs, oil, orange rind and juice together. Pour into the centre and beat well with a large wooden spoon. If the mixture looks a little dry, add some water. It should be soft but not runny – this can depend on the flours used.
5 Spoon into the cake tin, level off the top and bake for 1–1¼ hours until cooked, when a skewer inserted in the centre should come out clean.
6 Cool in the tin, upside-down, for an hour or so. Then remove the tin and peel off the Bacofoil. Leave to cool completely. Ideally, store the cake in an airtight tin for at least a day, because it will then be easier to cut, and will go further!

Curry Mango Yogurt

This is not only great for sneaking into, it is also extra-good dolloped onto the occasional small bowl of leftover rice or new potatoes; or, if you are feeling particularly virtuous, over a few leaves of crisp Cos lettuce.

1 large onion, chopped finely
1 garlic clove, crushed

1 tablespoon sunflower oil
2 tablespoons water
1–2 teaspoons curry powder, depending on strength
1 tablespoon mango chutney
250 g (8 oz) carton Greek yogurt or natural low-fat yogurt
1 tablespoon chopped fresh coriander or parsley
salt and ground black pepper

1 Gently sauté the onion and garlic in the oil and water for 10 minutes in a small covered saucepan.

2 Add the curry powder according to taste and fry, uncovered, for another minute. Remove and cool.

3 Blend in a food processor or liquidiser with the mango chutney, yogurt and herbs. Then season lightly. Spoon into a bowl and cover with Bacofoil or cling film. Best eaten within 3 days and not suitable for freezing.

No-cook Smoked Fish Pâté

Use any hot-smoked fish for this – mackerel, trout, Arbroath smokies – or even smoked salmon.

175 g (6 oz) smoked fish fillet, skinned, e.g. mackerel, trout, salmon,
   cooked kipper or haddock
4 spring onions, chopped finely
3 tablespoons low-fat spread
150 g (5 oz) carton of natural yogurt
1 teaspoon horseradish sauce
2 tablespoons chopped fresh parsley
2 tablespoons capers (optional)
ground black pepper

1 Check the fish for any bones. Then mash well with a fork.

2 Mix with the other ingredients until smooth. Spoon into a bowl or 500 g (1 lb) foil dish. Then cover with Bacofoil or cling film.

3 Alternatively, for a smoother pâté, blend everything except the capers in a food processor or blender, and stir in the capers, if used.

4 Store for up to 5 days in the fridge. This will freeze for up to a month, but wrap in Bacofoil, cling film or a freezer bag.

Mushroom and Toasted Almond Cream

If there is a vegetarian fridge-picker in the family, leave them a pot of this on the top shelf (plus a few vegetable sticks), and watch it disappear.

50 g (2 oz) flaked almonds
1 onion, chopped
1 garlic clove, crushed
2 tablespoons olive or sunflower oil
4 tablespoons water
250 g (8 oz) button or open-cup mushrooms, chopped roughly
2 tablespoons soy sauce
250 g (8 oz) curd or low-fat soft cheese
ground black pepper

1 Spread the almonds on your grill pan, and toast until nicely browned but not burnt.

2 Lightly sauté the onion and garlic in the oil in a medium saucepan for 3 minutes.

3 Add the water, mushrooms, soy sauce and pepper. Stir well, cover and simmer for 10 minutes, shaking the pan occasionally to stop the food sticking to the base. Try not to sneak a look, or you will let out the steam that is needed to cook the mushrooms without extra fat.

4 Allow to cool. Then blend in a food processor with the cheese and most of the nuts, reserving a few for garnishing if the mood takes you.

5 Spoon into a bowl, or 500 g (1 lb) foil dish and cover with Bacofoil or cling film. This is best eaten up within 5 days. It can be frozen for up to a month, but should be covered with Bacofoil or cling film, and needs a stir on thawing.

PICKERS' POPCORN

Instead of crisps, nuts or even more exotic nibbles, there's little to beat good old-fashioned popcorn. It's easily made in minutes, and it's best to eat it when it's freshly made. In a large, thick-based saucepan, heat 2 tablespoons of sunflower oil until a haze starts to rise. Add 3 tablespoons of popping corn, cover immediately with a lid, and cook on a medium heat without lifting the lid, shaking occasionally, until the popping stops. Season lightly if you must, but it's delicious without salt. Remove and nibble!

Tapenade (page 29)
No-cook Smoked Fish Pâté; Mushroom and Toasted Almond Cream

POWER-PACKED LUNCHES

A cut above the ordinary sandwich

More and more people in this country who eat away from home eat a packed lunch, including around a third of our school children. This number increases significantly each year.

Manufacturers and food retailers are taking account of this trend and are producing a greater and more interesting variety of suitable foods. The old attitude that a cold packed meal is 'not very good for you' is breaking down, as we realise that a well balanced meal does not have to be hot, filling, and eaten with a knife and fork. The temperature at which we eat our food matters not a jot, because it all becomes one temperature inside the tum anyway!

So if you and your family are great sandwich-eaters, or like eating with your fingers – carry on. But there is a danger with packed meals – the temptation to resort to using high-fat meats, pies and crispy snacks.This could well be because of the time factor: we are all rushing to get on with our lives. Instead of treating a packed meal as a quick snack to prepare as quickly as possible, think of it as a proper well balanced meal that needs as much planning as a sit-down meal. There are lots of highly nutritious foods ideal for out-of-the-home eating, as I hope these recipes will show.

Meals made up from the following list can be just as good as a 'proper hot meal': a well-filled sandwich or roll, a pot of salad, a yogurt, maybe some soup in the winter, a chicken drumstick or lean chop for adults and growing teenagers, fruit and maybe the occasional fun-size chocolate bar or a mini-box of dried fruit.

Three Salads Gone to Pot

Rice, pasta and pulses all make great one-pot packed meals, but they can be dry: the secret lies in dressing them while still hot in a vinaigrette, so they absorb flavour as they cool.

Serves 4

For the salad dressing:
2 tablespoons sunflower or olive oil, preferably extra-virgin
1 tablespoon wine vinegar
juice of ½ lemon
2 tablespoons water
1 garlic clove, crushed (optional)
1 teaspoon clear honey
1 teaspoon coarse-grain mustard
a pinch of mixed herbs
a little ground black pepper

1 Put everything into a screw-top jar and shake to mix.

Rice Salad

175 g (6 oz) brown rice
600 ml (1 pint) stock or water
1 bay leaf
2 spring onions, chopped
10 cm (4-inch) piece of cucumber, halved, de-seeded and chopped
1 large carrot, grated coarsely
50 g (2 oz) unsalted peanuts
2 eggs, hard-boiled and chopped
8 black olives, stoned and halved (optional)
2 tablespoons chopped fresh parsley or half a punnet of salad cress
salt and ground black pepper

1 Bring the rice and stock or water to the boil with the bay leaf. Then cover and simmer gently for 30 minutes or until cooked and the water is absorbed.
2 Toss in the dressing and allow to cool completely.
3 Mix with the other ingredients, seasoning to taste. Then divide into four picnic pots and cover with Bacofoil or cling film. Keep chilled until ready to pack.

Chicken Tikka Pittas

Truly a mouthful – in more ways than one. This recipe brings together two new ready-made foods sold fairly easily through supermarkets – pitta breads and chicken tikkas, those delicious bite-size nuggets of Indian spiced chicken.

Makes 4

4 mini-size or 2 normal-size pitta breads
250 g (8 oz) pack ready-cooked chicken tikka pieces
½ bunch watercress, de-stalked and leaves chopped roughly
4 small lettuce leaves, shredded
1 tablespoon reduced-calorie mayonnaise
2 tablespoons natural yogurt
1 tablespoon fresh chopped chives or spring onion tops
ground black pepper

1 Halve the mini pittas, or quarter the normal-size ones. Then carefully pull them open.
2 Cut the chicken tikka into thin slices and mix with the watercress, lettuce, mayonnaise, yogurt, chives or spring onions and pepper to taste. Salt should not be necessary.
3 Divide the mixture between the pittas and wrap each in cling film. Keep cool until ready to pack in lunch or picnic boxes.

Chicken Tikka Pittas

Pasta Salad, Rice Salad and Bean and Cheese Salad Gone to Pot

Turkey and Peanut Butter Sandwich
Sardine Sandwich
Brie and Walnut Sandwich
Avocado and Tomato Sandwich

Bean and Cheese Salad

**175 g (6 oz) dried beans, e.g. kidney, pinto, borlotti, butter, black-eyed, or
a mixture**
125 g (4 oz) green beans, topped, tailed and halved
½ small onion, chopped
1 red or green pepper, de-seeded and sliced
½ small bulb fennel, sliced thinly or 1 head chicory, sliced
50 g (2 oz) chopped walnuts (optional)
125 g (4 oz) hard cheese (ideally half-fat) cut into thin sticks
salt and ground black pepper

1 Soak and cook the beans according to pack instructions. Drain, toss in the dressing (page 39) and allow to cool completely.

2 Cook the green beans lightly in a small amount of water until just tender. Drain and toss with the cooked dried beans.

3 Mix with all the other ingredients, seasoning to taste. Divide between four picnic pots and seal with Bacofoil or cling film. Keep chilled until required.

Pasta Salad

250 g (8 oz) pasta shapes or macaroni
2 tomatoes
2 sticks of celery, sliced thinly
125 g (4 oz) frozen peas, thawed
3 spring onions, chopped
125 g (4 oz) button mushrooms, sliced
175 g (6 oz) cold, cooked and skinned chicken, diced
2 tablespoons flaked almonds, toasted
2 tablespoons fromage frais or natural yogurt (optional)
salt and ground black pepper

1 Cook the pasta in plenty of boiling water according to pack instructions. Drain and toss in the dressing (page 39). Allow to get quite cold.

2 Dip the tomatoes into boiling water for 30 seconds. Then remove and peel. Quarter, de-seed and slice.

3 Mix with all the other ingredients, seasoning to taste. Then divide between four picnic pots and seal with Bacofoil or cling film. Keep chilled until required.

Sandwich and Roll Fillings

Bread is now back in favour with nutritionists and cooks. Although regarded as a snack food until quite recently, a sandwich or filled roll is now seen as a good, balanced, light meal – provided the filling is not too high in fat. Bread contains good quantities of protein, starch (a carbohydrate), fibre (more in wholemeal), iron and vitamins of the B group.

Fresh bread is a must. If your family does not eat much bread at other times, either buy smaller loaves or freeze half a large loaf for later. Dried, stale bread is fine to eat healthwise, but one is tempted to add more butter or a fatty filling to compensate.

These sandwiches can be made in bulk and frozen as individual servings. Alternatively, they can be made the night before (this, incidentally, helps the flavour to develop). Wrap in Bacofoil (ideal because it keeps the bread and filling moist) or cling film, or put in food bags.

All these fillings are in one way or another nutritionally good, although those marked 🍴 are a little high in calories, so use sparingly.

☛ Smoked mackerel, chopped cucumber, horseradish and reduced-calorie mayonnaise.

🍴 Chilled, thinly sliced corned beef, the fat scraped off, topped with reduced-calorie coleslaw or juicy sliced tomatoes.

☛ Thinly sliced cold pork, with mango chutney and thick natural yogurt.

☛ Scrambled egg and Gentleman's Relish.

☛ Canned salmon, with thinly sliced celery, sweet relish and reduced-calorie mayonnaise.

☛ Sliced cold turkey or chicken, with peanut butter and cranberry jelly.

☛ Sardines mashed with lemon juice, capers and a sprinkling of dill.

Vegetarian Fillings

🍴 Vitality butties – mix together grated cheese, beansprouts, grated carrot, raisins and chopped unsalted peanuts. Spread in bread and spoon on a dressing of thick-set natural yogurt, clear honey and fresh lemon juice.

🍴 Avocado, sliced tomato and beansprouts.

☛ Thinly sliced tomato, mozzarella and cucumber in pitta breads.

🍴 Blue brie (softened) and walnuts – no butter with this one, as it is quite high in fat already.

☛ Mushroom and toasted almond cream from page 36 with extra thinly sliced raw mushrooms.

44

POWER-PACKED LUNCHES

Mexican Chilli Bean Soup

Warming, spicy and full of beans – this is an excellent, highly nutritious soup for packing into your family's flasks. Serve it with some wholemeal cheese rolls followed by fresh fruit, and the family won't go hungry until they get back home.

Serves 4–6

**1 onion, chopped
1 garlic clove, crushed
1 green or red pepper, de-seeded and chopped
1 large potato, unpeeled and diced
1 tablespoon sunflower oil
2 tablespoons water
1 teaspoon mild chilli powder
½ teaspoon ground cumin
400 g (14 oz) can of chopped tomatoes
1 litre (1¾ pints) stock
1 teaspoon oregano
1 tablespoon tomato purée or tomato chutney
425 g (14 oz) can of red kidney beans
200 g (7 oz) can of sweetcorn
salt and ground black pepper**

1 Gently cook the onion, garlic, pepper and potato in the oil and water in a covered saucepan for 10 minutes.

2 Add the spices and cook for another minute. Then stir in the tomatoes, stock, oregano, purée or chutney and seasoning.

3 Bring to the boil and simmer for 25 minutes. Add the beans and corn with their liquors and cook for a further 5 minutes. Pour into vacuum flasks while still hot.

Mexican Chilli Bean Soup; Date and Oaty Crumbles

Date and Oaty Crumbles

Makes 16

250 g (8 oz) pack stoned dates, chopped, if necessary
strips of peel and juice of 1 orange
300 ml (½ pint) water
100 g (3½ oz) granary or plain flour
100 g (3½ oz) wholemeal flour
100 g (3½ oz) sunflower margarine, plus extra for greasing
75 g (3 oz) quick porridge oats

1 Put the dates, orange peel strips, juice and water into a small saucepan and bring to the boil. Then turn down and simmer, uncovered, for about 10 minutes until soft and pulpy and the liquid is absorbed. Cool a little.

2 Preheat the oven to Gas Mark 5/190°C/375°F.

3 Rub the flours and fat together until resembling fine breadcrumbs. Then mix in the oats.

4 Line a 23 cm (9-inch) square tin with Bacofoil and grease lightly. Sprinkle half the crumble mix into the base and pat down to firm.

5 Spoon over the date pulp and smooth to cover the crumble mix. Then sprinkle over the remaining crumble and pat again to firm.

6 Bake for about 40 minutes until pale golden and firm. Cool in the tin for half an hour. Then turn out and cool further. Cut into 16 squares when quite cold and store in an airtight tin. Wrap in small pieces of Bacofoil when packing up for lunch or picnics.

Mix-and-match Quiches

Makes 2 × 20 cm (8-inch) flans, each serving 4

For the pastry:
125 g (4 oz) plain flour, plus extra for rolling
125 g (4 oz) wholemeal flour
125 g (4 oz) sunflower margarine
cold water
For the basic filling:
1 large onion, sliced thinly
1 garlic clove, crushed
2 lean rashers back bacon, de-rinded and chopped
1 tablespoon sunflower oil
2 eggs, beaten

300 ml (½ pint) skimmed milk
a good pinch of dried thyme
125 g (4 oz) half-fat cheese, e.g. Cheddar, Cheshire or Edam-type, grated
salt, ground black pepper and ground nutmeg
Optional fillings, per quiche:
1 medium courgette, sliced thinly and blanched
or 50 g (2 oz) button mushrooms, sliced thinly and blanched
or 3 tablespoons sweetcorn
or 6–8 small broccoli florets, blanched
or 125 g (4 oz) canned or cooked smoked fish, flaked, e.g. tuna, mackerel,
    salmon, haddock, etc.

1 Rub the two flours with the margarine until the mixture resembles fine breadcrumbs. Mix with just enough cold water to form a firm dough and knead until smooth.

2 Cover with cling film and allow to rest for half an hour.

3 Cut into two. Then roll each out on a lightly floured board to fit two 20 cm (8-inch) Alcan flan cases.

4 Trim the edges, if necessary, prick the base and leave to rest for another 15 minutes. Tear off two sheets of Bacofoil large enough completely to cover the flans. Fit them into the pastry cases, making sure the edges go over the top. Fill with baking beans and place on two flat baking sheets.

5 Preheat the oven while the flans rest to Gas Mark 6/200°C/400°F.

6 Bake the flans for 20 minutes, uncovering for the last 5 minutes and removing the foil and beans. Turn the oven down to Gas Mark 4/180°C/350°F.

7 Meanwhile, gently fry the onion, garlic and bacon in the oil in a covered saucepan for 10 minutes. Spoon into the flan. Add any other fillings of your choice, and sprinkle over the cheese.

8 Beat the eggs, milk, thyme and seasonings together. Slowly pour over the fillings and then bake for 40–45 minutes until golden and firm. Cool before cutting each into four.

9 To serve, wrap each piece separately in Bacofoil or cling film. Freeze spare sections until required, but use within 6 weeks. Put in lunch boxes, unwrapped, and thaw for about 2 hours.

POWER-PACKED LUNCHES

FAMILY FILLERS

Substantial meals for hungry hordes

Family meals are perhaps the easiest dishes gradually with which to change over to a healthier way of eating.

These recipes have less meat and fat and more fibre than the ones you may be used to: grains, pasta, potatoes and wholemeal flour are used a lot. You will find plenty of flavour here, too – using herbs, spices and small amounts of relish, chutneys and bottled sauces, it is possible to match the tastes you enjoy in less healthy foods.

Do try and cut down on salt, however – not all at once, or you will put the family off the whole idea before they have really started, but gradually. Start by adding smaller and smaller pinches to food in cooking. Always taste food anyway during cooking before seasoning – there may already be a lot from other ingredients. Then try occasionally 'forgetting' to put the salt cellar on the table – the chances are that the family won't miss it.

Quick Ginger Pan Chicken

Serves 4

1 onion, sliced thinly
1 garlic clove, crushed
2.5 cm (1-inch) knob of fresh root ginger, peeled and grated
1 small green pepper, de-seeded and sliced
2 tablespoons sunflower oil
500 g (1 lb) boned and skinned chicken breasts, sliced
3 strips of peel and juice of 1 lemon
300 ml (½ pint) chicken stock
1 tablespoon chopped fresh dill or 1 teaspoon dried dill
2 tablespoons chopped fresh parsley
3 tablespoons thick yogurt or fromage frais
salt and ground black pepper

1 Fry the onion, garlic, ginger and pepper gently in the oil for 5 minutes.
2 Raise the heat slightly and fry the chicken slices for about 3 minutes to brown.
3 Add the lemon peel, juice, stock and dill. Season, bring to the boil, and then simmer for 10 minutes, stirring occasionally. Stir in the parsley.

4 Off the heat, mix in the yogurt or fromage frais, stirring until smooth. Reheat very gently, without boiling, if necessary. There should, however, be enough heat already
5 Serve straightaway, with rice or pasta and a green vegetable such as mangetouts or beans. Remove the peel strips before serving.

Lean Beef and Lentil Shepherd's Pie

Serves 4

1 tablespoon sunflower oil
250 g (8 oz) lean minced beef or lamb
2 tablespoons water
1 onion, chopped finely
2 carrots, grated
2 sticks of celery, sliced finely
1 tablespoon wholemeal flour
600 ml (1 pint) stock
125 g (4 oz) red lentils
125 g (4 oz) button or open-cup mushrooms, sliced
1 large bay leaf
1 teaspoon dried marjoram, oregano or thyme
750 g (1½ lb) potatoes, cooked and mashed
a knob of low-fat spread
3 tablespoons dried breadcrumbs, preferably natural colour
salt and ground black pepper

1 Heat the oil in a frying-pan until very hot. Then fry the mince, stirring constantly, until browned. Add the water, then the onion, carrots and celery.
2 Cover and cook gently for 5 minutes until softened and then stir in the flour.
3 Add the stock, lentils, mushrooms, herbs and seasoning. Bring to the boil, then cover and simmer for 25 minutes. Remove the bay leaf and spoon the mixture into a pie dish.
4 Mix the mashed potatoes with some low-fat spread. Then spoon on top and fork attractively. Sprinkle with the breadcrumbs and brown under a medium-hot grill. Serve hot, with green vegetables or a salad.

FAMILY FILLERS

Marvellous Macaroni Cheese

A popular glutton's light supper dish, macaroni cheese can also be really good for you – especially if you can reduce the fat and increase the iron and fibre with spinach. The eggs and tuna are optional but make this dish more of a main meal. Watch out for the fat contents in different kinds of cheese – they vary.

Serves 4

250 g (8 oz) wholemeal pasta shapes
1 large onion, chopped
900 ml (1½ pints) skimmed milk
1 large bay leaf
2 tablespoons cornflour
250 g (8 oz) frozen leaf spinach, thawed
1 teaspoon coarse-grain mustard
75 g (3 oz) mature Cheddar or Edam cheese, grated
25 g (1 oz) grated parmesan cheese, preferably fresh
200 g (7 oz) can of tuna, drained well and flaked (optional)
½ teaspoon dried thyme, oregano or marjoram
2 eggs, hard-boiled and sliced (optional)
2 tablespoons wholemeal breadcrumbs
salt, ground black pepper and grated fresh nutmeg

1 Put the pasta, onion, milk and bay leaf into a large saucepan. Season lightly and bring to the boil, taking care the milk does not boil over. Lower to a gentle simmer and cook for 15–20 minutes or until the pasta is just tender. Remove the bay leaf.
2 Blend the cornflour with a little water and stir into the saucepan, until smooth and thickened.
3 Add the spinach and mustard and cook for another 2 minutes.
4 Off the heat, stir in the cheeses, the tuna (if used) and the herbs. Check the seasoning and pour into a large shallow heatproof dish. Arrange the eggs, if used, on top and scatter with the breadcrumbs. Brown under a preheated grill until crispy and serve immediately.

Roastabag Lamb Chops with Tomato and Aubergines

Serves 4

small aubergine, sliced thinly
onion, sliced thinly
small green pepper, de-seeded and sliced
tablespoons sunflower oil
400 g (14 oz) can of chopped tomatoes
grated rind and juice of 1 lemon
small sprig of fresh rosemary or ½ teaspoon dried rosemary
teaspoons flour
lean lamb chops, about 125–175 g (4–6 oz) each, e.g. chump, butterfly,
    shoulder, leg steaks
salt and ground black pepper.

Layer the aubergine slices in a colander and sprinkle lightly with salt. Stand the colander in a sink and allow any juices to drain for about 20 minutes. Rinse well; then pat dry with kitchen towel.

Preheat the oven to Gas Mark 4/180°C/350°F.

Fry the onion, pepper and aubergine slices gently in the oil in a large frying-pan, covering to keep the steam in. This helps the aubergines to soften without extra oil. Cook for about 10 minutes.

Add the tomatoes, lemon rind and juice and rosemary. Season lightly.

Shake the flour in a standard-size Roastabag (this stops any sudden splattering of hot fat). Then tip in the vegetables.

Lay the bag flat in a roasting pan and place the chops on top of the vegetables. Seal the bag with the tag provided. Then cut about 6 slits on top.

Bake for about 45 minutes or until the chops are tender. This is delicious with crusty bread to mop up the juices.

Note: This dish can be cooked ahead in the Roastabag, and then cooled and frozen. Thaw thoroughly before reheating, which can be done in the microwave or in a conventional oven.

Chopped Top Fish Pie

A creamy fish pie mixture covered with diced potatoes in skins.

Serves 4

500 g (1 lb) skinned and filleted white fish, e.g. cod, haddock, coley or whiting
250 g (8 oz) skinned and filleted smoked white fish
450 ml (¾ pint) skimmed milk
150 ml (¼ pint) dry cider
1 bay leaf
a handful of parsley stalks
1 tablespoon cornflour
250 g (8 oz) broccoli florets, trimmed
2 leeks, sliced
2 tablespoons chopped fresh parsley
750 g (1½ lb) potatoes, diced
1 tablespoon low-fat spread
salt, ground black pepper and grated nutmeg

1 Preheat the oven to Gas Mark 5/190°C/375°F.
2 Poach both the fish in the milk and cider, with the bay leaf and parsley stalks, for 1 minutes, until just cooked.
3 Remove the herbs, drain the liquor and reserve. Then flake the fish.
4 Blend the cornflour with a little water and mix into the drained liquor. Bring to the boil, stirring, until thickened. Season.
5 Blanch or steam the broccoli and leeks until just tender; drain well.
6 Arrange the fish in the dish; cover with the vegetables and sauce.
7 Cook the potatoes until softened but not mushy. Drain and toss in the low-fat spread. Spoon on top of the fish. Sprinkle over the nutmeg.
8 Bake for 35 minutes until the top is golden brown. Serve hot. There is no need for extra vegetables.

Note: This could be divided between two Alcan foil pie dishes for freezing. Cover with cling film or Bacofoil, seal and label, and use within six weeks. Unwrap and thaw before cooking as above, allowing an extra 10 minutes cooking time.

Bean and Beef Burgers

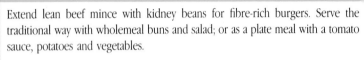

Extend lean beef mince with kidney beans for fibre-rich burgers. Serve the traditional way with wholemeal buns and salad; or as a plate meal with a tomato sauce, potatoes and vegetables.

Serves 4

125 g (4 oz) dried red kidney beans, or 425 g (14 oz) can of red kidney beans, drained well
3 tablespoons wholemeal breadcrumbs, if using canned beans
250 g (8 oz) lean minced beef
1 small onion, chopped finely
1 garlic clove, crushed
1 tablespoon soy sauce
1 tablespoon Worcestershire sauce
1 egg, beaten
1 teaspoon dried thyme or mixed herbs
a little sunflower oil
ground black pepper

1 If using dried beans, soak and cook according to pack instructions, making sure you boil them well for the first 10 minutes of cooking. Drain well and mash. Cool.
2 Mix with the other ingredients, except the oil. You should not need extra salt because of the sauces. Season with ground black pepper.
3 Shape into 4 large or 8 smaller, flattish patties.
4 Brush the burger tops lightly with oil, and also lightly oil the grill pan.
5 Preheat the grill and cook the burgers for 4 minutes on each side. Serve in toasted wholemeal buns with salad. Or make a quick home-made tomato sauce with chopped onion, garlic and a can of chopped tomatoes; serve with baked potatoes and vegetables.

PASTRY

Pastry *is* fattening, there's no getting away from it, but you can make it more acceptable by using at least half wholemeal flour and a sunflower margarine. Low-fat spreads don't make good pastry, though: edible but tough! In fact, one needn't cover the top of a pie with pastry. Roll out half your usual amount of pastry and cut out little shapes. Bake these separately and serve with casseroles or stewed fruit as croûtons. Same sensation – half the calories!

FAMILY FILLERS

Bigga Pizza Pie

When the family or a group of friends are all gathered together and look like they're hungry it's the right time to think Italian and roll out a pizza. It is actually simple to make an authentic one, and if the topping ingredients are prepared beforehand, the bread mix dough just needs mixing and a little proving.

Serves 4–6

1 large onion, sliced thinly
2 garlic cloves, crushed
2 tablespoons olive oil, preferably extra-virgin, plus extra for greasing
2 × 400 g (14 oz) can of chopped tomatoes
3 sun-dried tomatoes, chopped or 1 tablespoon tomato purée
½ × 567 g (1¼ lb) pack of brown bread mix
400 g (14 oz) pack of mozzarella cheese, sliced
50 g (2 oz) thinly sliced Italian salami or ham, shredded
about 12 pitted olives or 2 tablespoons capers
2 tablespoons chopped fresh parsley or oregano
salt and ground black pepper

1 Gently fry the onion and garlic in the oil for 5 minutes until softened.

2 Add the canned tomatoes, dried tomatoes (if used) or purée, and seasoning. Simmer for 10 minutes until slightly thickened. Cool.

3 Make up the bread mix, using half the pack and water. Cover the bowl with cling film and leave to prove until double in size. The time for this will depend on the room temperature, and the weather – anything from ½–2 hours.

4 Preheat the oven to Gas Mark 6/200°C/400°F, and lightly grease your largest baking sheet.

5 Knock back the dough. Then roll out to fit the base of the baking sheet. It does not matter if the shape is a bit irregular – this adds to the authentic look!

6 Spread over the tomato sauce, arrange the cheese on top (cut this with a wet knife), scatter over the salami or ham shreds, the olives or capers, the herbs, and some freshly ground black pepper.

7 Bake for 20–25 minutes until bubbling and cooked. Serve immediately.

Chicken Liver Risotto

A tub of frozen chicken livers is amazing value, especially as they take next to no time to cook. This recipe is a shining example of how healthy eating costs very little and tastes so good!

Serves 4

250 g (8 oz) brown or white rice
2 tablespoons olive oil, preferably extra-virgin, or sunflower oil
250 g (8 oz) chicken livers, thawed and sliced
4 rashers lean streaky bacon, de-rinded and chopped
2 courgettes, sliced
2 leeks, sliced
125 g (4 oz) button mushrooms, halved
½ teaspoon dried thyme
a good pinch of dried sage
2 tablespoons dry vermouth or sherry (optional but nice)
150 ml (¼ pint) stock
4 tablespoons fromage frais or natural yogurt
salt and ground black pepper

1 Cook the rice according to pack instructions. Then drain and rinse. Keep warm in a low oven.

2 Heat the oil and stir-fry the livers and bacon for about 3 minutes until firm and browned.

3 Add the vegetables and fry for about 3 minutes, sprinkling in the herbs and vermouth or sherry, if used. Cook for another minute.

4 Add the stock, bring to the boil and cook for another minute or two. Season, stir in the fromage frais or yogurt, and then the rice. Serve as soon as possible, with a salad and some crusty wholemeal bread.

Bigga Pizza Pie

ken Liver Risotto

Good Life Wheaty Pancakes;

Good Life Wheaty Pancakes

Serves 4

For the pancakes:
125 g (4 oz) wholemeal flour or half wholemeal, half plain
1 egg (size 2)
300 ml (½ pint) skimmed milk
a little sunflower oil

For the filling:
1 onion, chopped
1 garlic clove, crushed
175 g (6 oz) button mushrooms, sliced roughly
1 tablespoon sunflower oil
250 g (8 oz) frozen leaf spinach, thawed, squeezed dry and chopped
a good pinch of ground cumin or coriander
250 g (8 oz) cooked or canned kidney, cannellini or borlotti beans
50 g (2 oz) mature Cheddar or Edam cheese, grated finely

For the tomato sauce:
1 onion, chopped
400 g (14 oz) can of chopped tomatoes
2 teaspoons tomato chutney or relish
½ teaspoon dried thyme
salt and ground black pepper

1 Either put the flour into a bowl, make a well in the centre and gradually beat in the egg and milk until you have a smooth batter; or put all the batter ingredients into a food processor or blender and whizz to a batter.

2 Preheat a small omelette or frying-pan until really quite hot. Brush with just enough oil to coat the base lightly. Spoon in about 2 tablespoons of batter, swirling the pan immediately so the batter coats the pan base. You can tell if the pan is hot enough – it should give off a good sizzling noise.

3 Cook until the liquid mixture turns solid and bubbles appear. Flip over with a palette knife and cook the other side. Repeat with the rest of the batter until you have between 8 and 10 pancakes. Stack the pancakes up and keep them wrapped in a large piece of Bacofoil so that they remain moist and supple.

4 Preheat the oven to Gas Mark 5/190°C/375°F.

5 Now for the filling: sauté the onion, garlic and mushrooms in the oil in a covered saucepan for about 5 minutes until softened.

6 Add the spinach, spice and beans; then season lightly. Cook for about 3 minutes.

7 Lay the pancakes out on a board. Divide the filling between them and roll or fold them up. Arrange in a shallow casserole dish.

3 Put the sauce ingredients in a pan, bring to the boil and then simmer gently for 10 minutes until thickened and pulpy. Season lightly.

9 Pour the sauce over the pancakes. Sprinkle with the cheese and when ready to serve, reheat in the oven for about 20 minutes. Serve hot.

Baked Fish Steaks with Tasty Vegetables

Serves 4

2 carrots, peeled and cut in thin sticks
1 small bulb of fennel, sliced thinly
1 large leek, sliced thinly
2 tablespoons olive oil, preferably extra-virgin, or sunflower oil
4 fish steaks or cutlets, e.g. cod, salmon, halibut, conger eel – about 175 g (6 oz) each
3 tablespoons dry white wine or stock
2 tablespoons chopped fresh parsley or 1 tablespoon chopped fresh dill
3 tablespoons single cream
salt and ground black pepper

1 Preheat the oven to Gas Mark 5/190°C/375°F.
2 Blanch the vegetables lightly in fast boiling water for just a couple of minutes. Then drain, rinse in cold running water and toss in the oil.
3 Divide the vegetables between the fish steaks, season lightly and place in a Roastabag on a baking sheet.
4 Sprinkle over the wine or stock, herbs and cream.
5 Seal with the tag provided and bake for 25–30 minutes or until the fish feels firm and is cooked.
6 Remove the fish carefully from the bag with the vegetables still in place and pour any juices around. Serve with mashed potatoes and green beans.

VEGETABLES

Where possible eat these raw, to keep the maximum vitamins. Turnips, sprouts, and leeks are delicious grated raw and dressed with lemon juice; also, try grated raw courgette, beetroot, thinly sliced cauliflower and uncooked sweetcorn kernels. In fact, sweetcorn can be eaten as a nibble instead of peanuts or crisps.

FAMILY FILLERS

Steak and Kidney Creole

An exotic version of an old favourite – without any fattening pastry. Using quick-cook meats, this should be ready in just about half an hour.

Serves 4

250 g (8 oz) lamb's kidneys, skinned, cored and quartered
2 tablespoons wholemeal flour
2 tablespoons sunflower oil
175 g (6 oz) rump steak, sliced in thin strips
2 tablespoons of water
1 onion, sliced
1 garlic clove, crushed
1 green or red pepper, de-seeded and sliced
2 sticks of celery, sliced
400 g (14 oz) can of chopped tomatoes
2 tablespoons red wine vinegar
½ teaspoon dried basil
½ teaspoon dried thyme
a good pinch each of ground cloves and ground allspice
salt and ground black pepper

1 Toss the kidneys in the flour. Heat the oil in a large frying-pan and fry the kidney and steak strips until browned. Remove them with a slotted spoon.
2 Add the water to the pan with the onion, garlic, pepper and celery. Cover the pan and cook gently for 10 minutes, until softened.
3 Add the tomatoes, vinegar, herbs, spices and a little seasoning. Bring to the boil.
4 Return the meats, lower the heat to a simmer, and cook for another 10 minutes or so. Serve with pastry croûtons (page 54), brown rice, pasta or baked potatoes, and a green vegetable.

Tarragon and Mustard Chicken

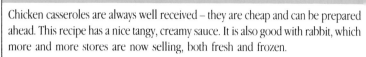

Chicken casseroles are always well received – they are cheap and can be prepared ahead. This recipe has a nice tangy, creamy sauce. It is also good with rabbit, which more and more stores are now selling, both fresh and frozen.

Serves 4

4 chicken quarters, skinned
2 tablespoons wholemeal flour
2 tablespoons sunflower oil
3 rashers lean streaky bacon, de-rinded and chopped
8–12 baby onions, peeled, or 1 onion, sliced
150 ml (¼ pint) dry cider
300 ml (½ pint) stock
1–2 tablespoons Dijon mustard
1 tablespoon fresh chopped tarragon or 1 teaspoon dried tarragon
3 tablespoons fromage frais or natural yogurt
salt and ground black pepper

1 Preheat the oven to Gas Mark 4/180°C/350°F. Toss the chicken portions in the flour.

2 Heat the oil in a frying-pan and brown the portions. Remove to a shallow ovenproof dish.

3 Fry the bacon and onions in the pan until browned. Then add the cider and cook until reduced by half. Stir in the stock, mustard, tarragon and some seasoning. Bring to the boil. Then pour over the chicken

4 Cover with Bacofoil and bake for about 1 hour, or until the meat is tender.

5 Stir in the fromage frais or yogurt, but do not reheat in case it curdles. Serve with pasta or cabbage sprinkled with a few caraway seeds.

DROOLERS' DELIGHT

Nice and not so naughty puddings

If your particular gluttony is a penchant for rich gooey, creamy puds, you are indeed unlucky. You are constantly first resisting temptation, and then giving in, and finally feeling guilty afterwards. Is it possible to be able to drool over healthy puds? Aren't they all dry, brown, and crying out for a jolly good dollop of thick luscious cream?

Well, try some of these recipes. They are all attractive, sweet, often creamy, and yet have been designed with health guidelines very much in mind. Please note, however, that they are *not* diet puds, just better for you than the usual calorie-crammed dessert or cake or biscuit!

EXERCISE

A healthy Glutton is well advised to keep fit – if only to help you enjoy your food more! And it doesn't take much time, either. But just like changing your food habits, don't try and charge straight into a strenuous exercise routine. Break yourself in gradually, even if you start by running down to the off-licence!

And you don't have to have been extra-good at school team games either. Many of today's popular exercises are ideal for the loner who was lousy on the school playing field. The maxim of 'little and often' is spot-on for the reluctant keep-fitter.

Fortunately, the most beneficial exercises can be done without having to book ahead for a partner or space in the gym. The best all-round exercise is swimming, followed by cycling, then brisk walking, jogging and running. For all these, start off slowly, doing as much at a time as you can without straining yourself, and then gradually build up, setting yourself personal bests which you can try and beat each week. If you feel faintly ridiculous at first, start in the early morning or at dusk when no one you know can quite see you.

When you begin to feel the benefits, which won't be long if you keep at it, start to treat yourself to rewards like a flop on the sun-bed, or (if you are female) a slinky pair of jeans, a new shorter skirt, or a make-up session at the local beauty shop.

Melon and Mango Salad with Lime Ginger Syrup

Why fruit salads have to be in glorious technicolour to be thought exciting, I will never know. The fruits should be good and ripe so there is no need to add sugar.

Serves 4–6

2 mangoes
1 medium-size melon, e.g. sweet honeydew or Galia, or 2 small ones, e.g. Charentais, or Ogen
2 kiwifruit
2 peaches or nectarines
1 star fruit (optional)
For the syrup:
½–1 × 250 ml (8 fl oz) bottle of slimline dry ginger ale
1–2 tablespoons whisky or ginger wine (optional)
To serve:
flower petals (optional)

1 Cut the mangoes down each side of the flat stone. Slash the flesh in lines through to the skin but do not cut the skin. Turn inside out and cut off the fruit in slices. Cut off the remaining fruit still on the stones. Discard the skin.

2 Halve the melons, de-seed, and scoop out in balls or chunks. Reserve any juices.

3 Peel and halve and slice the kiwifruit. Stone and slice the peaches or nectarines. Slice the star fruit, if used.

4 Mix everything in a large bowl. Pour over the ginger ale, according to your taste. Some people like a lot of syrup with their salads, others prefer theirs just moistened. Stir in any reserved fruit juices, together with the lime rind and juice and the whisky or ginger wine, if used.

5 Cover the bowl with cling film and leave in the fridge for the flavours to develop and mingle.

6 Turn out into your best glass bowl and scatter over some pretty flower petals like roses, chrysanthemums, tiger lillies, jasmine or primulas.

Hot and Honeyed Banana and Apple Kebabs

Here is a quite different way of serving fresh fruit. Make sure the fruits are ripe and naturally sweet.

Serves 4

1 orange
1 tablespoon clear honey
a pinch of cinnamon or mixed spice
2 large or 4 small ripe bananas
2 red apples

1 Pare the zest from the orange. Then scrape off any pith and cut the zest into fine julienne strips. Simmer these for 5 minutes in water to soften. Then drain and snip into short lengths. Return to the pan.
2 Squeeze the orange juice and add to the pan, together with the honey and spice. Heat gently until runny.
3 Peel the banana and cut into bite-size chunks. Core the apple and cut into the same sized chunks.
4 Thread onto skewers or wooden satay sticks. Put the kebabs on the grill pan.
5 Brush with the honey glaze, and grill on both sides for about 8 minutes, brushing in between until the glaze is used up. Serve immediately and try and resist any accompanying cream! If you must, make it a lower fat alternative like fromage frais or yogurt.

Not-so-guilty Profiteroles

It is possible to make light, crisp profiteroles using less fat than usual. So working on that basis, I thought, why not fill them with some juicy strawberries, top with a *small* dollop of cream, and simply trickle lightly with some hot chocolate sauce? Much better than the usual over-sickly, all-embracing coat.

Makes 8

For the choux pastry:
50 g (2 oz) plain flour
150 ml (¼ pint) cold water
40 g (1½ oz) butter or sunflower margarine, plus extra for greasing
3 eggs (size 2), beaten
For the sauce:
50 g (2 oz) bar plain chocolate
2 tablespoons hot water

½ teaspoon vanilla essence

For the filling:

250 g (8 oz) fresh strawberries or raspberries or 2 ripe peaches, stoned and sliced

150 ml (¼-pint) whipping or low-fat cream

2 teaspoons icing sugar (optional)

1 egg white

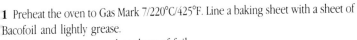

1 Preheat the oven to Gas Mark 7/220°C/425°F. Line a baking sheet with a sheet of Bacofoil and lightly grease.

2 Sift the flour onto another sheet of foil.

3 Put the water in a medium-size saucepan with the butter or margarine and slowly bring to the boil. By this time the fat should have just melted.

4 Immediately tip in all the flour. It helps to fold the Bacofoil in two to form a sort of funnel, so the flour shoots straight into the pan.

5 Beat vigorously until the mixture forms a smooth lump and comes away from the sides. Do not overbeat – stop when it is just smooth. Remove from the heat and cool for 10 minutes.

6 Off the heat, gradually work in the beaten eggs until the mixture is thick but not too soft and holds its shape. It should just drop from a wooden spoon when shaken, so you may not need all the egg.

7 Spoon or pipe eight blobs onto the Bacofoil-lined baking sheet. Bake in the preheated oven for 20–25 minutes until golden brown and quite crisp on the outside.

8 Slit through the middle and, using a teaspoon, scoop out any uncooked mixture on the inside. Return the choux buns to the oven for another 5 minutes to dry out even more. Cool on a wire tray.

9 In a small basin, over a pan of gently simmering water, melt the chocolate. Then mix in the hot water and essence. Remove from the heat and allow to cool until lukewarm.

10 When cool, slice the strawberries or peaches, and spoon the fruit of your choice into the centre of the buns.

11 Whip the cream until stiff with the icing sugar, if used. Then, using a clean whisk, whisk the egg white until stiff. Fold the two together. Then spoon this on top of the fruit.

12 Arrange on a large platter or on individual plates and trickle over the sauce. Serve immediately.

Note: The choux buns can be made ahead and then reheated in a warm oven until crisp again.

DROOLERS' DELIGHT

Little Devils' Food Cake

There is no such thing as a diet chocolate cake, but this is not quite as wicked as the full-blown version.

Serves 8–12
4 tablespoons cocoa powder
150 g (5 oz) dark brown soft sugar or molasses
5 tablespoons water
125 ml (4 fl oz) skimmed milk
50 g (2 oz) low-fat spread, plus extra for greasing
2 eggs, separated
1 teaspoon vanilla essence
150 g (5 oz) wholemeal flour
1 teaspoon cream of tartar
1 teaspoon bicarbonate of soda
1 egg white
5 walnut halves, to decorate (optional)
For the icing:
125 g (4 oz) icing sugar
2 tablespoons cocoa powder
1 teaspoon vanilla essence
1 tablespoon softened butter
2–3 tablespoons hot water

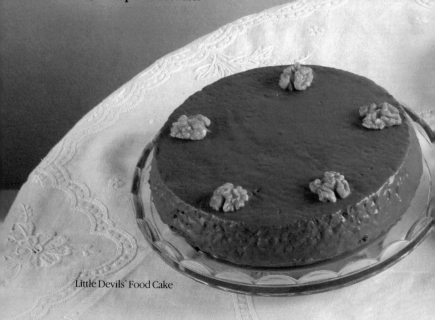

Little Devils' Food Cake

1 Preheat the oven to Gas Mark 4/180°C/350°F. Grease a deep 20 cm (8-inch) cake tin and line the base with lightly greased Bacofoil.

2 Blend the cocoa, 3 tablespoons of the sugar and the water until smooth. Beat in a small saucepan until thickened. Stir in the milk and cool.

3 Beat the low-fat spread with the remaining sugar until creamy. Then beat in the yolks and essence.

4 Sift the flour, cream of tartar and bicarbonate together. Tip any bran left in the sieve back into the flour. Then stir gently into the mixture with the cocoa milk.

5 Whisk the 3 egg whites until they form stiff peaks. Then gently fold into the mixture. Spoon into the prepared tin and bake for 40–45 minutes until firm to touch – a skewer pushed into the centre should come out clean.

6 Turn the tin upside-down on a wire tray to cool for about an hour. Turn out, peel off the Bacofoil and cool completely.

7 Sift the icing sugar and cocoa powder into a bowl. Beat in the rest of the ingredients until smooth. If needs be, add a few more drops of hot water, but the mixture should not be too runny. Spoon onto the cake top, and spread around the sides. Decorate with walnuts, if you wish.

Oh Go On Roulade

Not-so-guilty Profiteroles

Oh Go On Roulade

Now, I know chocolate roulade is the thing gluttons would kill for, but it is *really* high in naughty bits! However, it is possible to enjoy a light roulade with a nice gooey filling – this one has a creamy apple and damson one.

Serves 6

a little sunflower oil, to brush
2 eggs
50 g (2 oz) caster sugar
50 g (2 oz) plain flour
½ teaspoon mixed spice
For the filling:
1 large Granny Smith apple, peeled, cored and diced
grated rind of 1 small orange
1 teaspoon clear honey (optional)
a little water
125 g (4 oz) quark (semi-skimmed soft cheese) or low-fat soft cheese
3–4 tablespoons damson jam, warmed
a little icing sugar, to dust

1 Lightly oil a swiss roll tin, or alternatively you can make a suitable mould with Bacofoil as follows: tear off a sheet of Bacofoil about 40 cm (16 inches) long. Fold the edges in some 4 cm (1½ inches) all round. Then unfold and snip the little squares that have formed on the corners of the diagonal. Place this on a large flat baking sheet and lightly, but thoroughly, brush all over with sunflower oil. Now pull up the sides and shape into a shallow rectangular 'tin', securing the corners with 4 paper clips.

2 Preheat the oven to Gas Mark 5/190°C/375°F.

3 Whisk the eggs and caster sugar in a large bowl over a pan of gently simmering water until they are thick and creamy and the mixture leaves a trail on itself when trickled from the whisk. Remove it from the heat and continue to whisk for a minute or two longer.

4 Sift the flour and spice together. Then very carefully fold into the mixture.

5 Spoon into the prepared tin or case and level gently with a knife. Then bake for about 12 minutes until the sponge is golden brown and the top is springy when touched.

6 Meanwhile, wet a tea towel and lay it flat on a worktop. Lay a 40 cm (16-inch) length of Bacofoil on top and dredge lightly with icing sugar.

7 Turn the sponge out onto the sugary foil. Leave for a couple of minutes. Then carefully peel off the Bacofoil in strips.

8 Roll the roulade up with the sugary foil inside and the damp cloth outside. Do not roll the cloth into the sponge: it should just be used to wrap round the rolled-up sponge as it cools, to keep it moist.

9 Meanwhile, cook the apple with the orange rind, honey and a little water until soft and pulpy. Cool completely and mix with the quark or soft cheese.

10 Unwrap the roulade, spread the inside with the warm jam and then the apple filling. Re-roll, and do not panic if it cracks a bit – that is what makes it look so light and tempting. Dust over a little more icing sugar and serve as it is. No cream!

DROOLERS' DELIGHT

Autumn Fruits Crumble

A good mid-week pud, high in fruit and fibre and quite low in fat.

Serves 4

250 g (8 oz) blackberries, hulled, or a small can of berries in natural juice
2 ripe pears, cored and sliced
2 large sweet dessert apples, cored and sliced
1 tablespoon clear honey (optional)
½ teaspoon ground cinnamon
125 g (4 oz) unsweetened muesli
4 tablespoons bran flakes
grated rind of 1 lemon
2 tablespoons demerara sugar

1 Preheat the oven to Gas Mark 5/190°C/375°F.

2 Mix the fruits together, sweeten with honey if necessary, add the cinnamon, and simmer in a saucepan for about 10 minutes. Spoon into a 1-litre (2-pint) ovenproof dish.

3 Mix the muesli, bran flakes, lemon rind and demerara sugar together, and sprinkle over the fruits.

4 Bake for 15–20 minutes until the topping is crisp and golden brown. Serve warm with thick yogurt, or fromage frais, or even a little single cream.

Note: The base can be made in bulk during the autumn fruit glut and frozen in blocks. Then unmould and wrap in a freezer bag. Do not use a foil container, as the fruit acid could react with the foil.

Goody Goody Two Fruits Tart

Black and redcurrants are good high-fibre fruits, and, fortunately, high in flavour too.

Serves 6

For the pastry:
75 g (3 oz) wholemeal flour
75 g (3 oz) plain flour, plus extra for rolling
75 g (3 oz) sunflower margarine
a little cold water
For the filling and topping:
175 g (6 oz) blackcurrants
175 g (6 oz) redcurrants
2 tablespoons of water
about 2 tablespoons sugar, or to taste
125 g (4 oz) quark (semi-skimmed milk soft cheese) or fromage frais
2–3 teaspoons clear honey
grated rind of 1 lemon
2 tablespoons redcurrant jelly (optional)
a few mint leaves, to decorate

1 Mix the flours in a bowl. Then rub in the margarine until it resembles fine breadcrumbs. Mix to a firm dough with just enough cold water – do not make it too wet or the pastry will be tough. Allow to rest for 15 minutes.

2 Roll out on a lightly floured board to fit a 23 cm (9-inch) flan tin. Trim the edges and prick the base. Rest again for 15 minutes and preheat the oven to Gas Mark 6/200°C/400°F.

3 Line with a sheet of Bacofoil and some baking beans. Then bake blind for 20 minutes, removing the Bacofoil and beans for the last 5 minutes to let the pastry crispen. Cool.

4 Trim the fruits of any stalks, and stew in water, with the sugar to taste, for about 15 minutes. Drain carefully and cool. Reserve a tablespoon of the juice and keep the rest for a refreshing drink later.

5 Mix the cheese or fromage frais with the honey and grated rind until smooth. Then spread on the flan base.

6 Spoon the fruits on top. Melt the jelly with the reserved tablespoon of juice and then trickle over the fruits. Decorate with a few mint leaves if you like.

Goody Goody Two Fruits Tart; Autumn Fruits Crumble

Wholesome Strawberry Tartlets

I devised this recipe very late one night, when I remembered it was my children's sports-day the next day. I had not made my contribution to the parental tea table, and all I had in the fridge was a punnet of strawberries and a tub of soft cheese past its sell-by date. I am pleased to say, the tarts all vanished within minutes, and since then I have *had* to make them on many other occasions, for fear of family mutiny.

Makes 18
For the pastry:
125 g (4 oz) wholemeal flour
125 g (4 oz) plain flour
2 tablespoons icing sugar
125 g (4 oz) sunflower margarine or low-fat spread
about 3 tablespoons cold water
For the filling:
200 g (7 oz) tub of low-fat soft cheese
1 tablespoon set honey
1 teaspoon vanilla essence
about 250 g (8 oz) fresh strawberries (around 18), sliced
a little icing sugar
leaves of fresh mint or maidenhair fern, to decorate

1 Stir the two flours and icing sugar together in a bowl. Then rub in the margarine Mix to a firm dough with cold water. Knead lightly. Then wrap in Bacofoil or cling film and chill for about 30 minutes.

2 Preheat the oven to Gas Mark 5/190°C/375°F.

3 Roll out quite thinly on a lightly floured board and cut out eighteen 7.5 cm (3-inch) rounds, re-rolling if necessary. Fit into tartlet-size patty pans. Prick the bases twice with a fork, and chill again for 15 minutes.

4 Bake for 12–15 minutes until golden brown. Then remove to a wire tray to cool and crisp.

4 Mix the cheese with the honey and essence. Then spoon into each tartlet case and level off.

5 Slice the strawberries and arrange attractively on top of the cheese. Dust lightly with a little icing sugar tapped from a small sieve, and decorate with sprigs of mint or fern. These tartlets can be made a few hours in advance and kept chilled until ready to serve.

Wholemeal Toast Ice Cream with Hot Blackcurrant Sauce

125 g (4 oz) wholemeal breadcrumbs
3 egg yolks
2 eggs
175 g (6 oz) light brown soft sugar
300 ml (½ pint) milk
300 ml (½ pint) single cream
1 teaspoon vanilla essence
For the sauce:
200 g (7 oz) can of blackcurrants in natural juice
1 teaspoon cornflour
2 teaspoons cassis or crème de menthe

1 Grill the breadcrumbs until lightly toasted, moving them about occasionally. Cool.

2 Beat the yolks, eggs and sugar in a bowl.

3 Scald the milk, cream and essence in a saucepan until just on the point of boiling.

4 Pour from a height onto the egg mixture, beating with a wooden spoon. Strain back into the saucepan and, on the lowest heat possible, stir the custard constantly until it thickens slightly. Do not overheat or it will curdle. If it shows signs of doing so, plunge the pan into a bowl of cold water (it might be a good idea, if this is your first custard, to have one at the ready).

5 Cool, then chill. Stir in the breadcrumbs and pour into a shallow freezerproof bowl.

6 Freeze until slushy. Then take out and beat well. (This is best done in a food processor, if you have one.) Return the mixture to the freezer and refreeze. Again, when slushy, give it another beating. Spoon it back into the bowl and freeze until solid – several hours. Cover with freezer cling film, seal and label. Use within 2 months.

7 Thaw for about 20 minutes in the fridge before serving.

8 For the sauce, drain the juice from the fruit and blend it with the cornflour. Heat in a saucepan (or in a jug in the microwave), stirring until smooth. Add the cassis or crème de menthe and the blackcurrants, and reheat.

DROOLERS' DELIGHT

Banana and Blackcurrant Ice

Two high-fibre fruits, mixed with honey and yogurt, make a simply delicious and healthy ice cream.

Serves 4–6

500 g (1 lb) fresh blackcurrants or 2 × 200 g (7 oz) can of blackcurrants in natural juice
3 tablespoons clear honey
2 large ripe bananas, peeled and sliced, plus more to sprinkle
75 g (3 oz) sugar
500 g (1 lb) Greek or low-fat natural yogurt
2 egg whites
desiccated coconut, to sprinkle (optional)

1 If using fresh currants, strip them from their stalks and stew gently for 5 minutes in 150 ml (¼ pint) water. Then cool.

2 Put the currants into a food processor or liquidiser and blend until smooth. Then add the honey, bananas, sugar and yogurt.

3 Pour into a shallow freezerproof container. Chill and then freeze until nearly frozen. Remove from the freezer and beat until slushy.

4 Whisk the egg whites until they form soft peaks. Fold into the slushy mixture and return to the freezer. When frozen, wrap in Bacofoil or cling film, or pop the container into a large freezer food bag. Seal and label. Use within 3 months. Thaw for 20 minutes, before serving in scoops. Sprinkle with the coconut and banana slices if you wish.

Wholemeal Toast Ice Cream with
Hot Blackcurrant Sauce

Banana and Blackcurrant Ice

Wholesome Strawberry Tartlets

FEASTS

Festive food for family and friends

There are times when we either want to (or have to) eat a really good slap-up meal.

Should you feel guilty? Only if you genuinely want to lose weight. The problem with large special-occasion or family get-together meals, is that people feel that in order for them to be tasty and delicious, they must be full of fat, sugar or salt or a combination of these. In fact, it is possible to eat well and enjoy a delicious meal that, if not exactly slimming, is still full of foods that will do you good in some form or other. The golden rule, as with all sensible eating, is not to go over the top: moderation and balance in all things. So, enjoy your occasional binge – after all, eating is supposed to be a pleasure.

Sunday Lunch Lamb and Potato Curry

Since the days of the British Raj, a leisurely curry lunch has been traditional on certain Sundays, if only to revive memories for old colonials. Actually, such a lunch can be much leaner than a full-blown roast with all the trimmings, but still leaves you feeling nice and drowsy afterwards. Another advantage is that the curry is best made the day before and simply needs reheating, while the accompaniments can be prepared ahead, popped in their serving bowls and covered with Bacofoil or cling film – so you can really enjoy your Sunday lie in. You don't even have to lay a table – the guests can stand or sit on the floor because it can all be eaten with just a fork.

Serves 4–6
4 tablespoons desiccated coconut
600 ml (1 pint) hot stock or water
2 garlic cloves, chopped roughly
5 cm (2-inch) cube of fresh root ginger, peeled and sliced roughly
2 green chillies, halved, de-seeded and sliced roughly
2 teaspoons cumin seeds
1 tablespoon coriander seeds
1 tablespoon fennel seeds
2 teaspoons fenugreek seeds (optional)
2 tablespoons sunflower oil
500 g (1 lb) lean boneless lamb, neck fillet or leg, cubed

1 large onion, peeled and sliced
1 dried red chilli, crushed (optional)
1 stick of cinnamon, halved
4 cloves
5 cardomom pods
750 g (1½ lb) potatoes, cubed·
1 tablespoon mango chutney
425 g (14 oz) can of chick-peas, drained
1–2 teaspoons garam masala power
salt and ground black pepper

1 Soak the coconut in the hot stock or water for at least an hour. Drain, discarding the coconut.

2 Preheat the oven to Gas Mark 5/190°C/375°F.

3 Crush the garlic, ginger and green chillies in a pestle and mortar, or pulverise in a blender or food processor.

4 Put the cumin, coriander, fennel and fenugreek seeds, if used, on a baking sheet, and roast in the oven for 5–7 minutes. Cool and crush these. If you haven't a pestle and mortar, roll them hard on a board with a rolling pin.

5 Heat the oil and brown the meat for about 3 minutes, turning once or twice. Remove it with a slotted spoon.

6 Fry the onion and garlic mixture gently for 3 minutes. Then add all the spices, including the whole ones but excluding the garam masala. Fry for a minute or two.

7 Stir in the coconut stock and bring to the boil. Return the meat to the pan, with the potatoes, chutney and seasoning.

8 Cover and simmer gently for about 50 minutes, until the meat is tender and the potatoes have broken down a little and thickened the sauce.

9 Add the chick-peas and garam masala. Continue simmering for a further 10 minutes. Ideally, cool, transfer to a heatproof dish and cover with Bacofoil or cling film ready to reheat the next day. When reheating, make sure that the mixture bubbles well for about 5 minutes.

Cucumber Raita

Coarsely grate half a cucumber, put it into a colander and sprinkle lightly with salt. Leave to drain for 20 minutes. Rinse well and pat dry. Then mix it with 2 finely chopped spring onions, 2 tablespoons of chopped fresh mint (or 1 teaspoon of dried), 250 g (8 oz) of natural thick-set yogurt, and seasoning.

Other Bits on the Side

Half the fun of a curry lunch is all the pretty side dishes. Make up a selection of about six from the following, laying them out on small plates or bowls and covering with foil or cling film until ready to serve.

- ☛ Chopped mixed peppers: red, green and yellow.
- ☛ Chopped raw onion (spanish onions are less strong).
- ☛ Chopped hard-boiled egg.
- ☛ Chopped apple sprinkled with fresh lemon juice and mixed with a few raisins.
- ☛ Toasted desiccated coconut.
- ☛ Roasted unsalted peanuts or cashew nuts or flaked almonds (but remember that these are high in calories).
- ☛ Chopped tomato and celery or fennel.
- ☛ Sliced banana, sprinkled with fresh lemon juice.
- ☛ A basket of freshly toasted poppadums, allowing two per person.
- ☛ A choice of chutneys – mild and sweet and hot and spicy.

Beef Estoufade

A well balanced diet contains a great variety of foods which can include red meats such as beef, venison or lamb. Make sure these are lean and in moderate amounts. Red meat is a valuable source of iron.

Serves 8

750 g (1½ lb) lean braising beef or venison, cubed
250 g (8 oz) lean shoulder of pork, cubed
3 tablespoons wholemeal flour
2 tablespoons sunflower oil
2 garlic cloves, crushed
2 tablespoons of water
375 g (12 oz) baby onions, peeled
300 ml (½ pint) dry red wine
300 ml (½ pint) beef stock
2 tablespoons tomato purée
a sprig of fresh rosemary
a sprig of fresh thyme
2 bay leaves
250 g (8 oz) button mushrooms
125 g (4 oz) small black olives
salt and ground black pepper
chopped fresh parsley, to garnish

1 Preheat the oven to Gas Mark 2/150°C/300°F.
2 Toss the meats in the flour in a food bag.
3 Heat the oil in a large frying-pan and brown the meats, with the garlic, for about 5 minutes. Remove to a casserole dish with a slotted spoon.
4 Add the water to the pan and fry the onions gently for 5 minutes, turning occasionally, until lightly browned.
5 Pour in the wine, scrape up any meaty deposits, and bubble up for a few minutes. Add the stock, tomato purée, herbs and some seasoning. Bring to the boil and pour over the meat.
6 Cover tightly, first with a sheet of Bacofoil, and then with a lid, to ensure a good fit. Bake in the oven for about 2 hours, or if you are using venison, for about 2½ hours.
7 Uncover and add the mushrooms and olives. Then re-cover and return to finish cooking for a further half-hour. When tender, serve sprinkled with the parsley, accompanied by crisp, green vegetables or a salad, and the Garlic and Olive Bread on page 88.

Pork with Orange Ginger Vegetables

This is a rolled, easy-carve joint cooked on a bed of vegetables in a Roastabag, so all the juices make a tasty gravy. You could use rolled veal, or lamb, or a breast of turkey instead; pork, is, incidentally, a good source of Vitamin B.

Serves 6–8

1.5 kg (3½ lb) rolled lean pork, without rind
1 garlic clove, cut in slivers
1 tablespoon flour
2 sticks of celery, sliced thinly
2 parsnips, peeled and chopped
2 carrots, peeled and sliced thinly
2 leeks, sliced thinly
12 no-soak dried apricots, halved
grated rind and juice of 1 orange
150 ml (¼ pint) stock or water
2 teaspoons cornflour
a little cold water
salt and ground black pepper
1–2 tablespoons chopped fresh parsley, to garnish

1 Preheat the oven to Gas Mark 4/180°C/350°F.
2 Stab the joint a few times and stick in the slivers of garlic. Shake the flour in a large Roastabag.
3 Mix all the vegetables together, with the apricots, orange rind, juice, stock or water and some seasoning. Then pour into the bag.
4 Place the joint on top of the vegetables, loosely secure with the bag tag, and stab the top of the bag a few times to allow the steam to escape.
5 Roast for 1½–1¾ hours until the meat is tender. Allow to stand for 10 minutes.
6 Snip a corner off the bag and strain the juices into a small saucepan, then spoon off any fat. Carve the meat and arrange with vegetables on a platter. Sprinkle with the parsley.
7 Mix the cornflour with a little cold water and stir into the pan juices. Bring to the boil, stirring until the gravy thickens. Serve the gravy separately. This is good with some crisp, green vegetables or red cabbage, and baked jacket potatoes.

Salmon with Twenty Leaves of Bay

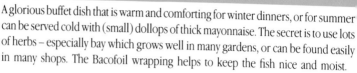

FEASTS

A glorious buffet dish that is warm and comforting for winter dinners, or for summer can be served cold with (small) dollops of thick mayonnaise. The secret is to use lots of herbs – especially bay which grows well in many gardens, or can be found easily in many shops. The Bacofoil wrapping helps to keep the fish nice and moist.

Serves 8

1 whole salmon, about 2 kg (4½ lb), gutted
3 tablespoons olive oil, preferably extra-virgin
around 20 large bay leaves
1 small handful of fresh basil leaves or 1 teaspoon dried
1 medium-size onion, sliced thinly
1 lemon, sliced thinly
150 ml (¼ pint) dry white wine
salt and ground black pepper

1 Preheat the oven to Gas Mark 5/190°C/375°F.

2 Tear off a sheet of Bacofoil two-and-a-half times the length of the fish. If you do not have a large oven, you may need to cut the fish head off. Lightly brush the Bacofoil down the centre with a little of the oil.

3 Scatter one-third of the bay and basil leaves, onion and lemon slices on the base. Lay the fish on top.

4 Fill the body cavity with another third of the leaves, seasoning lightly.

5 Arrange the rest of the herbs on top. Fold over the Bacofoil, pouring over the wine as you fold, so that it does not run out. Then roll the ends to seal.

6 Lift the fish onto your largest baking sheet or roasting pan and bake for about 50 minutes or until the fish feels firm along the backbone which indicates that it is cooked. To double check, lift some of the skin and see – it should flake and look pale pink.

7 Allow to cool still wrapped in Bacofoil even if you intend serving it hot – let it stand like this for 20 minutes. The fish can be skinned, but nowadays it seems the fashion to leave the nice shiny skin on – which is one less job for you.

Note: This recipe would also work wonderfully with a sea-bass, although it may cost you half as much again as a salmon.

Lentil Lasagne Loaf

Serves 4

8 sheets of lasagne
1 large onion, chopped
2 garlic cloves, crushed
2 tablespoons sunflower oil, plus extra for greasing
1 small bulb of fennel, chopped
125 g (4 oz) red lentils
3 tomatoes, skinned and chopped
300 ml (½ pint) vegetable stock or water
250 g (8 oz) frozen leaf spinach, thawed and squeezed dry, then chopped
125 g (4 oz) ricotta or medium-fat curd cheese
50 g (2 oz) grated parmesan cheese, preferably fresh
salt, ground black pepper and freshly grated nutmeg

1 If necessary, boil the lasagne sheets according to pack instructions. Rinse them well and drain on kitchen paper towel. If you are using no-cook lasagne, dip it briefly into boiling water to soften it.

2 Preheat the oven to Gas Mark 4/180°C/350°F.

3 Lightly grease a 1 kg (2 lb) loaf tin and line the base with Bacofoil.

4 Gently fry the onion and garlic in the oil for about 7 minutes to soften. Remove half and reserve.

5 Add the fennel to the pan and cook for 5 minutes.

6 Add the lentils, tomatoes, stock or water and seasoning. Bring to the boil; then cover, and simmer for about 25 minutes until pulpy.

7 Mix the reserved onion with the spinach and reheat briefly in a separate pan. Then stir in the ricotta or curd cheese. Season and add a little nutmeg.

8 Arrange about 3 lasagne sheets on the base and sides of the loaf tin to overhang slightly.

9 Spoon some spinach filling on the base, sprinkle over some parmesan cheese and cover with lasagne, cutting to fit as necessary. Spoon over some of the lentil filling, sprinkle on parmesan, and cover with more lasagne.

10 Repeat the layers until you reach the top of the tin, finishing with pasta. Fold over the lasagne pieces at the top. Reserve some parmesan for serving. Cover with some more lightly greased Bacofoil and bake for 30 minutes. Allow to stand for about 10 minutes before easing the pasta away from the tin sides and turning out.

11 Serve with home-made tomato sauce (see Good Life Wheaty Pancakes, page 58) and a crunchy green salad. It's also good with Garlic and Olive Bread (page 88).

Game Casserole with Orange and Juniper

Generally speaking, game, as long as it is lean, is low in saturated fats, and like other dark red meats, it is high in trace elements such as zinc, iron and copper. So when you can get it (and this is easier to do now, as much more is being farmed), treat yourself and your family or friends to some. Although I've specified hare or venison, wood pigeon or mallard are equally suitable, although you have to allow more per serving, because of the bones.

FEASTS

Serves 6

750 g (1½ lb) lean venison or hare, cubed or cut in chunks
2–3 tablespoons wholemeal flour
2–3 tablespoons sunflower oil
1 large onion, sliced
2 sticks of celery, sliced
50 g (2 oz) lean back bacon, de-rinded and diced
2 tablespoons red wine vinegar
about 10 juniper berries, crushed
2 bay leaves
grated rind of 1 orange
450 ml (¾ pint) stock or water
175 g (6 oz) button mushrooms
salt and ground black pepper

1 Preheat the oven to Gas Mark 4/180°C/350°F.
2 Toss the meat with the flour in a food bag. Heat 2 tablespoons of the oil in a large frying pan and quickly fry the meat until brown, for about 3 minutes. Remove.
3 Add extra oil, if needed, and fry the onion, celery and bacon for about 5 minutes.
4 Add the vinegar, and simmer until evaporated; then add the juniper berries, bay leaves, rind and stock or water. Stir well and bring to the boil.
5 Season lightly and spoon into an ovenproof casserole. Cover and cook for about 1 hour. Add the mushrooms. Return to the oven for a further ½ hour or until the meat is tender.
6 Serve with lovely, smooth, mashed potatoes mixed with some mashed swede or turnip, and some steamed, crisp, green or red cabbage.

Garlic and Olive Bread

This is a lighter and healthier version of a great favourite. Garlic bread is usually dripping in butter; this one, however, is lightly brushed with olive oil and spread with a black olive paste.

Serves 6

1 long french loaf or wholemeal baguette
2–3 tablespoons extra-virgin olive oil
2 garlic cloves, crushed
2 tablespoons black olive paste or 125 g (4 oz) black olives, stoned and chopped very finely
2 tablespoons chopped fresh parsley

1 Preheat the oven to Gas Mark 2/150°C/300°F.
2 Slash the bread about 12 times. Lay the pieces on a large sheet of Bacofoil.
3 Heat the oil and garlic in a small pan until they are just on the point of boiling.
4 Brush on one side only of the bread slices, making sure some garlic is included. Then spread some olive paste or the chopped olives on top. Sprinkle over the parsley and wrap the slices up in Bacofoil.
5 Bake in the oven for 30 minutes.

Garlic and Olive Bread

il Lasagne Loaf

Game Casserole with
Orange and Juniper

Rice-and-cashew-stuffed Turkey

A turkey is ideal for big family get-togethers when you want to push the boat out, without leaving your family and friends with that sinking feeling afterwards. Serve with some lovely crispy baked potatoes, and a large bowl of mixed salad.

Serves 8

3.5–4.5 kg (8–10 lb) turkey, thawed well if frozen, and with giblets reserved
For the stuffing:
175 g (6 oz) uncooked brown rice
1 onion, chopped
1 stick of celery, sliced
1 carrot, grated
50 g (2 oz) smoked back bacon, de-rinded and chopped
1 tablespoon sunflower oil
75 g (3 oz) cashew nut pieces, toasted
75 g (3 oz) sultanas
1 teaspoon mixed herbs
1 egg, beaten
2 tablespoons chopped fresh parsley
salt and ground black pepper
To roast the turkey:
sunflower oil, for brushing
ground paprika pepper
dried mixed herbs

1 Untruss the bird and clean with kitchen paper towel. Chop the liver and heart. Use the remaining giblets to make stock for the gravy.
2 Boil the rice according to pack instructions; drain and reserve.
3 Gently fry the vegetables and bacon with the chopped liver and heart in the oil, for 10 minutes, stirring occasionally.
4 Mix with the rice and rest of the ingredients, seasoning lightly. Allow to get cold before stuffing the bird.
5 Spoon into the body cavity, but don't pack it too tightly. Spoon also under the neck skin. Retruss the bird and place in a roasting pan.
6 Brush the skin with more sunflower oil and sprinkle with paprika and herbs.
7 Cook *either* covered in Bacofoil at Gas Mark 4/180°C/350°F for 3¼–3¾ hours, uncovering for the last half-hour to brown, *or* in a large Roastabag at Gas Mark 3/160°C/325°F for 2½–3 hours.
8 Test to see if done by sticking a thin skewer into the bird's thigh where it joins the

body. Clear juice should run out; if it does not, return the bird and cook until it does. Turkeys, like all meats, carve better if left to stand for 15 minutes, covered with a large clean sheet of turkey-size Bacofoil to retain the heat.

9 The pan juices can be added to the giblet stock to make the gravy, but do try and spoon off as much fat as possible, and thicken the meaty deposits with wholemeal flour. Also, turkey skin may well be delicious, but it is quite high in fat, so ration yourself to a small piece.

Crispy Roast Potatoes

Roast potatoes are a must for Sunday lunches. If you really do want to be healthy, then serve baked jacket potatoes, but, once in a while, a crisply roasted potato or two does you no harm.

I like to use a good-quality olive oil for special-occasion roasting, for the flavour, but a polyunsaturated sunflower oil is even healthier. The secret is to try and cut down on the amount of fat absorbed and to roast at a high temperature. If this is difficult because you have not got a cooker with a smaller top oven, then cook the joint first. Then wrap it in a double thickness of Bacofoil. You can leave the skins on the potatoes, if you wish. Cut them into even-sized pieces (about the size of a small apple). Par-boil them to cut down on the oven time. Make sure the oil is really hot, too, and brush it over rather than spoon it, so that you can get a lighter and more even covering.

Allow 3 servings per 500 g (1 lb) of potatoes, peeled and cut in even-size pieces. Boil in unsalted water for 5 minutes and then drain.

Preheat the oven to Gas Mark 6/200°C/400°F and then heat a thin film of olive or sunflower oil in the tin until it is very hot. Tip in the potatoes and brush the tops with the hot oil. Sprinkle lightly with garlic or celery salt and return to the oven for about 45 minutes, turning once, until they are all golden brown and crispy. Drain on kitchen paper and keep warm, uncovered, so that they remain crisp.

BOTTOMS UP

Cocktails and low-alcohol drinks

We all know that we should limit our consumption of alcohol, but gluttons are gregarious folk – they like to mix and socialise; and this can lead to one drink too many.

A moderate amount of alcohol will do most of us no harm and, taken sensibly, alcohol can help one relax and so reduce stress and tension.

A report by the Royal College of Physicians in 1986 recommended safe upper limits of alcohol consumption per week, measuring it in units.

1 unit is equivalent to 8 g of alcohol – that is, approximately half a pint of beer, one-third of a pint of cider, or 1 small sherry. A large glass of wine (red or white) is about 1½ units.

Consider the recommended safe upper limits per week and see how you do.

☛**Men** 21 units a week, with 2–3 alcohol-free days a week.

☛**Women** 14 units a week, also 2–3 alcohol-free days a week.

So how can we spin out the units and what can be served instead? Sweet softies are for sissies – what are needed are less sweet adult drinks, without alcohol or very much reduced in alcohol.

Fortunately there is now a good and increasing range of mineral waters, water and juice mixes, low-alcohol beers, and wines – in addition to the traditional alcohol-free mixers such as tonic, dry ginger and so on. Serve them on their own, or mix them with each other – as in '*LA shandy*'; low-alcohol beer with lemonade. Or try '*Pink tonic*', a good substitute for a gin and tonic – shake some angostura bitters into a glass, top with tonic and squeeze in a quarter of a fresh lime or lemon. Tonic water is also very good with a small amount of dry vermouth, and there is a sherry on the market for mixing specially with tonic water.

Spritzers or wine coolers are light wines diluted with sparkling mineral water or fruit juice or both. You can make your own, to taste, or buy ready-made versions which many wine departments and stores now sell.

You can make some very attractive home-made drinks that are low in alcohol, yet taste delicious. Try some of the following recipes.

Alcan Icebags

When you have run short of ice cube trays or you cannot find one that easily relinquishes its frozen nuggets, Alcan Icebags are a great boon. Each bag holds about 450 ml (¾ pint) water and several can be frozen at once.

☛ They are particularly useful for making mineral water ice cubes, using sparkling water that has gone flat, when you want to keep your water pure. The same goes for flat tonic or dry ginger – why dilute your drink with water?

☛ Use them for freezing strained stocks, so that you can add just a few for a small amount of stew or gravy.

☛ Make dolly-size lollies, to eat with a teaspoon, from fruit juices. Children seem to find these a novelty.

☛ Left-over wine can be poured in, ready for when you want to perk up an everyday stew or dish with just a splash or two of wine.

Whole Bitter Lemonade

Makes 1.2 litres (2 pints)
3 whole lemons, scrubbed and chopped roughly
2–3 tablespoons sugar
a few sprigs of fresh mint or 1 tablespoon angostura bitters or one sprig fresh rosemary
lemon slices and rosemary sprigs, to decorate

1 Grind the chopped lemons in the blender or processor with the sugar and just a small amount of water. When you have a good slushy mixture, slowly add about 600 ml (1 pint) of cold water and blend again.
2 Strain the juice through a sieve, pressing down well with a wooden spoon or the back of a ladle.
3 Return the pulp to the machine with the flavouring of your choice and add another 600 ml (1 pint) of water. Whizz up, then strain and press for a second time. Discard the pulp. Chill the lemonade until ready to serve.
4 Fill tall glasses with ice cubes. Pour in the lemonade and decorate with more thin slices of lemon and herb sprigs, if appropriate.

BOTTOMS UP

Party Sangria

Makes about 18 glasses
1 litre (1¾ pints) orange juice, preferably freshly squeezed
2 litres (3½ pints) dry red wine
2 oranges, sliced thinly
1 large lemon, sliced thinly
2 apples, cored and sliced
2 peaches or nectarines, stoned and sliced
2 cinnamon sticks, halved
icing sugar
1–2 litres (1¾–3½ pints) soda or mineral water or lemonade
ice cubes

1 Mix the orange juice and wine with the fruits, cinnamon and a little icing sugar to sweeten lightly, in a large bowl. Cover with cling film and chill for about 4 hours.
2 To serve, top with water or lemonade to taste and serve with lots of ice. Sip through straws.

Iced Fruit Tea Punch

Makes 18–20 glasses
175 g (6 oz) light brown soft sugar
1 litre (1¾ pints) strong hot tea
1 litre (1¾ pints) apple or orange juice
juice of 3 lemons
1 litre (1¾ pints) dry ginger ale
250 ml (8 fl oz) rum (optional)
ice cubes
fresh mint and fruit slices

1 Dissolve the sugar in the hot tea and allow to cool.
2 Mix with the rest of the ingredients and chill.
3 Serve over ice cubes and decorate with mint leaves and fruit slices.

INDEX

Design: Ken Vail Graphic Design
Photography: Eric Carter
Food preparation for photography: Roz Denny
Typesetting: Goodfellow & Egan Limited, Cambridge
Printed and bound in Great Britain by The Eagle Press, Blantyre

THE AUTHOR

Roz Denny is a freelance cookery consultant and writer. She has written numerous other recipe books, and contributes regularly to magazines.